Praise for *Mourning and Celebration*

"David Brody has carved a story with grace and sensitivity about a subject that some of us, still to this day, cannot even whisper: homosexuality. This deeply affecting story about a man trying to find his place in a world that has no place for him is a triumph. By writing this book, the author has made this story human and personal, making it impossible for us to ignore or shun gays and lesbians. From a perspective of a hundred years ago, we see just how far we have come to accept sexual orientation within society and religious constructs, but sadly, it reveals how far we need to go. More importantly, this novel transcends the barriers of religious denominations because the book is doing just that, breaking down barriers. It is not only a book for the Jewish faith but for all religions. David Brody has written this story with honesty and love, and I was very touched by it."

Cary Lawrence, actress, Montreal, Canada

"Well written with sensitivity. An enjoyable albeit heart-rending account of the ignorance shown in the past that has given way to the acceptance and liberal views of the present day. Although I have finished the book, Yankl's torment continues to live on in my mind."

Irene Chipchase, homemaker and booklover, Cambridge, UK

"I have just read your book. I couldn't leave my computer - and I cried again! Thank you for sharing this with me and indeed the world. God bless you, dear friend."

Carole Rocklin, fund-raising professional, Montreal, Canada

"David Brody in his new novel, Mourning and Celebration, vividly recreates the world of Eastern European Jewry in the nineteenth century before it was decimated by the Holocaust. With an authenticity that reminds us of Isaac Bashevis Singer, he draws readers into his narrative. Brody holds their interest by asking the following questions:

"What if a problem that we think of as new and modern has actually existed for a very long time? How did people who could not fit into the traditional societies of old find a place for themselves in the world?

"Today we are used to seeing gay people in all walks of life and we assume it is something new and characteristic of our own time. But what if gay people were finding a place for themselves in society for centuries? How might they have done this?

"These are the questions that Brody has answered with a story that is beautifully conceived and gracefully written."

Rabbi Howard Handler, Solomon Schechter School of Westchester, New York

"An elderly holocaust survivor once shared with me that when he was a boy his father took him to shul on Yom Kippur, and in the last row of the pews he saw a number of strangers, men without talesim weeping. He asked his father who those men were, and his father said, "they are the reshoim", wicked men. His portrayal of what it was like for Jewish gay men in 1930s Poland has made me hungry for stories like David Brody's. We are in need of a history that cannot be recovered. He has broken that silence with the first of stories that can only be imagined."

Rabbi Steven Greenberg, Director of the Diversity Project and Senior Teaching Fellow at CLAL (National Jewish Center for Learning and Leadership), Scholar-in-Residence for Hazon, a Jewish Environmental organization, and for Keshet, an organization dedicated to GLBT (gay, lesbian, bisexual and transgender) inclusion in the larger Jewish community

"I am sure Mourning and Celebration will be a great success. The story is amazing and brilliantly devised. It has both meaning and a message relevant today."

Lily Frank, former National Executive Vice-President, Canadian Hadassah/WIZO

"This story is an intelligent and soulful insight into a conflicted world that most neglect to imagine even existed. It is a story of pain and exploration, and it is a story in which the deeply human struggles are, tragically, timeless. I am grateful to consider the author a friend and my teacher in the implications of what transpires when deep emotional longing meets moral blindness."

Rabbi Adam Scheier, Congregation Shaar Hashomayim, Westmount, Quebec, Canada, the author's congregational rabbi

"This book is truly a gift bestowed upon its readers. One can only be grateful to the author for his generosity of spirit in sharing a journey so rarely revealed. Love propels us through time and tradition, all the while exacting a terrible price on wonderfully endearing characters. I read this book very slowly. I didn't want it to end."

Pauline de Waele, Administrator, Health Services, Montreal, Canada

"Danny (Rabbi Prof. Daniel Sperber, Chana's husband) and I are truly impressed by your writing. The story is so powerful and touching and sensitively told in exquisite English. I hope to see Yankl on screen soon. It would be amazing and a real mitzvah as a movie."

Chana Sperber, counselor to the parents of gay men and lesbians, Tel Aviv, Israel

"I read this book with extreme pleasure and great interest. I admire the warmth and dignity of the writer expressed so well on a theme with which he is so familiar."

Muguette Myers, Translator and published poet, Montreal, Canada

"David Brody has, in 'Mourning and Celebration,' attempted to fill in one of the many silences of gay and lesbian history, and in so doing has written a stirring tale that can open hearts. Brody imagines a counterpoint to himself: a young man in the shtetl whose love is denied him by the conventions and strictures of his time, and in this way calls us to ponder the thousands - perhaps millions - of people who are similarly bound today. Like the movie "Trembling Before G-d," this book gives human form to their struggle."

Jay Michaelson, Executive Director, Nehirim (USA): GLBT Jewish Culture & Spirituality, and author of "Everything is God: The Radical Path of Nondual Judaism"

"David Brody has written a powerful and sensitive story about human love as it was and is experienced by gay men with a vibrant spirituality, shaped by the traditions of the Jewish faith. In a most imaginative way, David imagines an encounter between himself today and a Chassidic Jew named Yankl, who lived more than a century earlier. Yankl's story of his wrestling with the conventions of his day, with his family's expectations, and with the demands of his orthodox faith, while refusing to deny his own sexual leanings, is fictional but totally believable and emotionally moving. And David Brody's own contemporary musings as a gay man and practicing Jew show that, in many ways, the struggle goes on. Though written from a Jewish perspective Mourning and Celebration has insights of great worth for anyone, gay or straight, who is struggling to remain faithful to themselves and to the spiritual tradition to which they may belong."

The Rev. Dr. Donald F. Bell, Minister, The United Church of Canada, Toronto, Canada

Mourning and Celebration

Jewish, Orthodox and Gay
Past & Present

With best wishes
K. David Brody

Visit Us Online!

The reading experience doesn't have to end with the book that you hold in your hands! On our website, you'll find:

- ✓ Information about K. David Brody, the author
- ✓ Reviews – read what others have to say, and submit your own!
- ✓ Speaking events – K. David Brody might be speaking in your area
- ✓ Frequently Asked Questions about the story and history surrounding it
- ✓ An easy way to tell your friends about this book, and share the experience with them!
- ✓ Contact information – send emails direct to K. David Brody!

We'd love to see you online, and look forward to hearing your feedback.

www.MourningAndCelebration.com

Mourning and Celebration

Jewish, Orthodox and Gay
Past & Present

K. David Brody

Cover design by Lauren Trimble Designs:
www.LaurenTrimble.com

ISBN 144868238X

If you would like to invite the author to speak at an event for your organization, please contact him via the website.

To the thousands of voiceless souls whose anguish could rise only to heaven.

Foreword

The author and I were at school together. I knew him as a somewhat reclusive individual, and also a very talented pianist. I had no idea of the personal anguish he was going through. At that time, I had little or no knowledge of such things, and he apparently concealed it well.

Times have changed, and even among Orthodox Jews, there is a growing understanding of the tragic situation in which a religious homosexual finds himself. There is a greater willingness to view the phenomenon with sympathy, rather than cause the "gay" to be an outcast, a pariah in his own community.

This new understanding is the direct outcome of clear articulation on the part of the "sufferer" as to his suffering, the "unfairness" thereof, and the living lie to which he may be doomed. Outspoken revelation of such a condition, brave and public, is a necessary element in the reevaluation of homosexuality in Jewish society, and society in general. Orthodox Jewish law has to contend with additional challenges, which may appear to be insoluble, but certainly evoke, nay mandate, empathy and kindness, and full admission into the community.

It takes great courage to step "out of the closet", and personal documentation of the trials and tribulations along this very difficult and perilous path will play a major role in righting the wrongs done to this socially misunderstood group of individuals.

We should be truly grateful to the author for opening a window onto his life, and perhaps unwittingly, making us feel guilty for our own lack of sensitivity.

Rabbi Prof. Daniel Sperber
President
The Ludwig and Erica Jesselson
Institute for Advanced Torah Studies
Bar-Ilan University
Ramat Gan
Israel

Author's Note

The writing of Mourning and Celebration has been a fascinating experience. The work is the birth child of two sources: a sense of self-awareness and a response to a historical dilemma that, to this day, has not been resolved – the place of homosexuals within Orthodox Jewry.

The characters in my book illustrate this dilemma. In the process, they seemed to take hold of my imagination and emerge on their own, my words serving merely as a mouthpiece for their description and development. My objective in embarking on this project was to use their story to seek recognition and understanding of the problem. Once that is achieved, minds much wiser than mine can devise a solution. That is my hope and prayer.

In order to explain the Yiddish and Hebrew words essential to the telling of the tale, I have added a glossary that redefines each word or phrase after it is first mentioned.

I would like to acknowledge with much gratitude the people who helped me produce this work. First, my sincere thanks to the clergy, professionals and friends kind enough to provide the testimonials validating my work. I am most thankful for their time and encouragement.

The ongoing, constructive comments of the Creative Writing Group of Westmount, Quebec, led by Alexina Scott-Savage, were much appreciated and had a radical effect on the shape of my novel.

My editor and publicist, Danny Iny, also made a significant contribution by correcting my language and advising me on how to get the book most effectively into your hands.

A word of thanks, too, to the many friends who read the work before I decided to 'go public', and who made suggestions that sparked the progress of the story.

Finally, a wish: that you enjoy reading Mourning and Celebration almost as much as I enjoyed writing it. Thank you.

K. David Brody

BOOK 1

Prologue

"Hey, *Lady*, catch this one!" The fair-haired boy stood arrogantly with two leering schoolmates. He bounced a tennis ball hard on the ground, its drumming on the asphalt a violent challenge in itself. He turned to his friends. "Let's see the little queer squirm."

"See if you can hit him where it counts," said the one with acne all over his face.

"Yeah," parroted the third member of the trio. "Where it counts."

"C'mon, then. Catch it if you can," yelled the fair-haired boy at the butt of his scorn.

He made a feint of hurling the tennis ball at his flinching target a few yards away in the schoolyard, and then flung it with all his strength. I, the object of his venom, scarcely had time to brace myself and turn away before the hurtling tennis ball struck me hard on the left shoulder blade. I winced with pain as, to the jeers of my tormentors, I slunk to the side of the schoolyard, once more the damage to my dignity more painful than the bruise to my back.

I recall the incident with dread whenever bullying is mentioned in the news or in newspaper articles. It is so far in the past, yet such grotesque memories still surface in my mind's eye as I relive those awful moments and remember my hurtful nickname. With a dislike of sports and a feeling of abhorrence at the very idea of competition – sports and competition being the fundamentals of grammar school culture in the London of the 1950s – I was humiliatingly dubbed *Lady*.

All I wanted was to be left in peace, and the only form of competition I sought was to surpass my own past record.

As I expel the unwelcome memory from my consciousness, I reflect on how circumstances have changed in my own lifetime. My youth was characterized by a sense of alienation from the society and values in which I grew up. Mine was the second generation of Jews to be born in London, England, my paternal grandparents having hailed from Poland and my maternal grandparents from the Ukraine. Life had been a struggle for my parents and their generation, born into poverty but rising through their efforts and some calculated risk-taking to a position of relative comfort. Yet the ghetto values of my grandparents had withstood the economic and social pressures to attain material success: what mattered most were family and the practice of Orthodox Judaism.

From the age of nine, I knew I was different. By the age of twelve, I realized what the difference was. With fear and horror I admitted to myself that I was attracted to my own sex. I desired boys. I had crushes on boys. Yet I felt most at ease around girls with whom there was no sexual tension and no fear of exposure. At the same time, I had little in common with them. Isolation and loneliness were the only option. Worse still was the terror of discovery, not to mention my parents' high expectations of me. How would they react? How could I ever fulfill their greatest hope for me – marriage and children? There would also be little chance of being accepted by others for what I was, a homosexual. At school I was persecuted for being different and for my feminine ways. I made great efforts to change those gestures and attitudes by practicing what I took to be masculine mannerisms. Indeed, I have succeeded to such an extent that, as an adult, I project the image of a typically straight male. I'm a closet heterosexual – a thought that creases my face into a grin.

Casting aside the memories, I realize that I managed to change my life. In 1968, by exchanging my place of birth for Montreal through emigration to Canada, I achieved liberation.

For many years, I enjoyed emotional satisfaction with a lover and a certain professional and economic success. And within my short lifetime attitudes have changed, from oppression and suspicion of gay people to quasi acceptance. Years ago, Jews were subjected to the same process: from the ghetto to emancipation, at least in day-to-day life. On a superficial, social level, being Jewish is accepted, despite some underlying anti-Semitism. And now, being gay almost does not matter. It's just a detail in one's personal character, a reality accepted as a normal part of life, especially in the province of Quebec.

Sometimes I wonder what kind of a person I would have been had I been born at another time and in another place. I'm quite sure that I'm not the first person to have made this conjecture, but that does not make the hypothesis any less intriguing. In fact, although my parents were London-born Jews, had they been Hindu Indians, how would I have grown up and developed? Or Mayan Indian? Do those societies accept a man who is homosexual? Completely homosexual? There are endless possibilities: a Lapland family? Inuit? Chinese? Then there is the time consideration. The worst-case scenario would have been as the only son of a Viking chieftain, obliged to perpetuate the family name. I imagine myself leaping off a cliff in a gesture of defiance. How dramatic!

It is an existential question, but there is one possibility well within the realm of the imagination. Had I been born 100 years earlier, at a time when my ancestors lived in ghettos or in *shtetls*, Jewish villages, to parents with a similar worldview to that of my own parents, how would I have reacted? How would they have reacted? Shtetl society was a fortress against external influences. Conformity was the rule – anything less would have been considered a threat to the status quo. Everyone dressed the same and thought the same – along strict Jewish religious lines. Non-conformity was anathema. How would I have survived in that totally closed, totally conformist society?

From my own chair in the comfortable living room of my apartment, I contemplate the social progress that has been made during my own lifetime. In my teenage years in London and in most other places in the world, the practice of homosexuality was illegal. I remember contributing small sums to an organization dedicated to law reform called the Albany Trust. It was founded after the Wolfenden Commission recommended amendment of the law in the UK prohibiting homosexual acts.

The Albany Trust issued a newsletter, sent in a plain brown envelope. I dared not receive it at home for fear that my parents would question me about it, and my secret would be revealed. So I asked a female friend at the college I attended to take delivery of the newsletter. She was consumed with curiosity as to the envelope's content and years later I regretted not having taken her into my confidence.

In Canada, I myself was involved in changing the status quo. When Yves, my lover of 23 years, passed away, I and three other gay men in the same situation sued the provincial government for the survivor pension, an allowance already granted to the surviving spouse in a common-law relationship. We were represented by a lawyer from the Quebec Human Rights Commission. After an eight-year legal battle, and with the case finally being considered by the Quebec Court of Appeal, the province's highest legal authority, we won our case.

Not bad, I think as I look across at the armchair facing me. Yet I'd give anything not to have had to claim the pension. The chair I'm looking at is the one Yves used to sit in, often waving his hands in animated conversation with me or our guests. It's just one of the many furnishings that carries a memory in the space I conceived. The style, Queen Anne, with a high back covered in velvet stripes of blue, ivory and olive, reflects both Yves' taste and his character, easy and elegant. Almost every other article in the décor represents a souvenir of an event or a mood, the earliest being a crystal egg I noticed by chance in the store window of Liberty's on Regent Street, London as I sheltered from a downpour. Love at first sight. It cost me the third of a week's salary, an expense I never regretted. It has accompanied me wherever I resided in the three countries I have lived in.

The massive sofa with its plush, blue cushions is another of Yves' pieces I inherited. Taking one's seat in it is to sink into a cloud. Elsewhere, placed carefully in the corner cabinet is my mother's Japanese tea and coffee set, hand-painted on paper-thin bone china, all too fragile ever to use.

My paintings, my loves. The calm riverside scene by a French painter from Provence, its magic light reflecting even in darkness. The rich fall colors of a Canadian forest, a watercourse trickling through it, by an artist from the Outaouais region of Quebec – the hues fade or glint with the intensity of the light shining on it. The stark lines of a mountain waterfall and lake portrayed by a European immigrant who, like me, forged his future in the New World. A still life hangs above the dining table by a young man from China. The beautiful 19th-century print of a man's head, discovered on a vacation in Burgundy. Knick-knacks on the piano, each echoing its innate occasion and its own beauty. My Sabbath candlesticks and my *chanukiyah,* the eight-branched candelabra, lit on the festival of *Chanukah,* to celebrate the rededication of the Temple after the Hasmoneans' victory over the ancient Greeks.

Taken together, my very own refuge.

Sometimes, on a sleepless night, I come into my sanctum, switch on one or two picture lights, sit in Yves' chair and contemplate the peace that permeates the place. When I first set eyes on the apartment, before I purchased it, there had been a full-sized pool table in the room with its overhead light, two little tub chairs and a small television suspended from the ceiling next to the French doors leading to the balcony. Nothing else. The walls had been covered in wallpaper with a dark green stripe. It was a depersonalized space more akin to a club than a residence, more suited to an amorphous group of guests than a homeowner's nest. I had changed the wallpaper for one with soft columns of winding brown leaves set against a beige background, lending height to the eight-foot ceiling in the front part of the room. However, the element opening up the space is a cathedral ceiling over the dining area, elevating the room from what would otherwise have been a box-like hutch.

Memories. Inanimate objects, each with their own history, relevant to me alone. When I am gone, they will have to survive on their own empty esthetic, subject and victim to others' tastes. When I am gone, my history, too, will be gone. Some friends and family will recollect events and occasions we shared. Then, they too, will vanish with time.

I suddenly become aware of my own thought process. Until recent years, I was almost exclusively preoccupied by my personal life situation, my daily problems insignificant as they may have been, and the long-term challenges that I have now learned to face and accept as part of my being. I realize that, in spite of my concerns, I have reached a certain comfort level, a serene plateau where the peaks and abysses of existence have been eroded to a flat plain. It is not a disturbing realization. I now have the space to observe and absorb other realities, the realities of others, and even other times. I cannot imagine what a projection of my life might hold for me 100 years hence. But the past? I have acquired enough knowledge to visualize that.

I close my eyes, picturing an ancestor sitting there, someone just like I had been years ago – lonely, isolated, alienated and desperate as a result of being gay. I'm sure someone like me must have existed and I feel an overwhelming affinity with this stranger from another world, this long-lost cousin.

I open my eyes. The chair is no longer empty. Sitting there is a Chassidic Jew, long-legged and lanky, dressed in a white shirt and black pants under a black smock. Around his waist is a black cloth belt, the *gartel,* separating his spiritual upper body from the lower part containing the bodily functions. His head covering is a *shtreimel*, a wide-brimmed, round fur hat. His face is framed by a trim beard with curly side locks swept back over his ears. His soft brown eyes are frightened, the eyes of a hunted animal. I know that feeling and that look, for before the western world changed, I had felt and looked the same way.

I stare at this apparition in disbelief. "Who are you?"

"Mein nomen is Yankl (Jacob) Bradawka. Or at least, Yankl was the name given to me at birth." The Yiddish accent is thick. "I am your cousin… I was your cousin," he corrects himself.

"My cousin? That's impossible."

"Nein, it is possible," says this cousin from another century and another culture.

"You mean we're from the same family but from a different time and place?" I pause, mulling over the intriguing situation. "Strange," I continue, "how could that be? Yet I always wondered whether you existed. I have often tried to imagine what it must have been like to be you. How different our lives must have been! Was it as awful as I think? Tell me what it was like."

Yankl removes his hat and places it in his lap. Beneath it he wears a black *yarmulkah,* the skullcap worn by religious Jews. Despite his strong Yiddish accent his English is clear and correct.

"It's quite a story. Quite a story," he muses. "I grew up in Rypin, in north central Poland, but I was not like the other boys there. I looked the same and dressed the same, but was not the same. Nobody knew how I felt. Nobody could see how I felt. I had secret desires, forbidden urges – strong sexual drives that I prayed no one would ever discover. I felt unique, worse than unique. A freak. The only one of my kind on earth. How was I to make my parents, sisters and friends happy? They expected so much of me that I could not deliver. I lived in a 19th-century shtetl but I desired other men. Yet another man could never give me a home and children. It was hell on earth." Yankl's face freezes as he relives the memory. He lifts a hand to his face, covering his eyes, as if in mourning for his own life.

My heart swells with compassion. What can I say to comfort this man? Can I explain that things will change a century and a half in the future? That the civilized world finally realizes what we both always knew: that 'choice' in our sexual orientation is not an option? Would that even be comforting? Perhaps just offering an empathetic ear might help.

"Please, Yankl, tell me about it. Tell me how you survived," I say.

"I lived a nightmare," Yankl replies. "It started in the local *yeshiva,* the seminary for Jewish boys." Yankl casts his mind back to those days of study, when he denied reality. He thought he was sick, and that like many sicknesses, it would just go away. In every other way, he functioned normally, but occasionally he still dared to hope that somehow, someone could feel as he did. As his teen years slipped by, he felt increasingly isolated. It seemed there was nobody with whom to share his feelings, nobody to whom he could speak openly.

Chapter 1

The hum of the students in the study hall wafted to the ceiling, the sound combining with the musty smell of old books and the slightly acrid aroma of young male bodies. The study hall or *yeshiva* was the place where nearly all the young men of Rypin spent most of their waking hours. Weak light filtered into the large room from windows set high in the walls. Oil lamps shed light on the Talmudic texts studied by the students, and all the young men of the village were there because nobody would have thought of going anywhere else. Some of the young men took time off in the afternoons to learn their father's trade, but all educational and social contact was centered around the study hall.

The young men studied in couples, each partner known as a *chevrusa*. They read passages from the Talmud, discussed them, cited different sources, and even tried to draw conclusions on how to lead their own lives from the words on the page; and everything was recited in the peculiar sing-song typical of religious study.

Yankl's chevrusa was Eliyohu. The two were the same age, 18, and had grown up together although they lived at opposite ends of the small town. Together, they had attended the *cheder*, the Jewish school for children. Later, aged thirteen, they had marked their *bar mitzvah*, the Jewish coming-of-age ceremony, in the same year, chanting the Torah portion of the week before the congregation; and then they had graduated to the yeshiva where they became chevrusas.

As Eliyohu grew, he became more attractive. Unlike most of his peers, his hair was a sea of blonde waves, spilling over his forehead. He had green eyes and an aquiline nose topping full lips that curled upward into a constant smile. His face was covered in a light blonde down that would soon develop into a full beard. Every day, Yankl looked forward to seeing him with far more enthusiasm than he had for study. He watched him, swaying gently as he intoned the sacred text of the Talmud.

"Rav Shimon says..." Eliyohu chanted. Yankl tried to concentrate. The text was something about a partnership between vintners. "Rabbah said..." Eliyohu continued. Yankl's mind drifted. How he would like to hold that head in his hands, kiss the forehead, the eyes, the nose and the lips! Walk hand in hand through the nearby forest.

"Yankl... Yankl!" Eliyohu was calling him. "What are you thinking about?"

Yankl jumped out of his daydream. "Nothing, nothing. I was miles away. Where were we?"

Eliyohu reached over the desk and turned Yankl's volume of the Talmud toward him, searching for the place. The print was so small that he had to put his finger on it for Yankl to see where they were. He returned Yankl's book to him, his finger still pointing to the relevant text. Yankl took the book and used his own finger to mark the place. Their hands touched. Yankl looked up; Eliyohu quickly withdrew his hand and turned away. He, too, had been aware of the moment when their fingers touched. But for him, touching another man was permissible only in terms of Chassidic dancing in the synagogue or at a wedding. Had he mistaken the feeling? Perhaps. Study was the only answer. He returned to chanting the text, his voice slightly too loud, his swaying slightly too energetic. "Rav Shimon says..."

Yankl noticed the change. There was no hope. Loneliness engulfed him as he took over reading aloud. His eyes absorbed the Aramaic text and his voice spoke the words. But there was no meaning to them. No sense. He read by rote, seeing himself in his mind's eye flying upward and backward, away from Eliyohu into blackness, while Eliyohu continued to immerse himself in the abstruse dictates of the Talmud.

The day of study drew to a close with the fading light. The young men gathered for the afternoon and evening prayers. As he stood with the others, Yankl looked around. Was he completely unique? Did anyone else in the entire world feel as he felt? Where were they, people like him? Did they exist? How to find them? Would they dare? Would he dare? What to do?

Yankl's eyes returned to his prayer book, the *siddur*. The *sh'moneh esray,* the silent prayer, recited standing, had begun. Yankl intoned the verses quietly, his mumbled words joining those of the young congregants, rising toward the ceiling. He reached the prayer for the healing of the sick. As always, he changed the words...

"*Ribonnoh shel olam,* master of the universe," he whispered, "make me well. Take away this curse that you have cast upon me. Why did you not make me blind, or deaf or dumb? People understand that. But this, they cannot. Give me, I beg of You, a desire for women. Answer my prayer, not for my sake, but the sake of my dear parents who have such high hopes for me. Grant me a wife and children to continue the name of our esteemed family. And give me peace of mind."

He had to speak to someone about this. Perhaps Eliyohu. Yes, given the right circumstances, Eliyohu. Yankl could talk to him about it.

Yankl walked home, passed the humble wooden dwellings of the shtetl, smoke curling skyward from the stoves cooking the evening meal. He considered his predicament. Isolation was his major problem. Perhaps God would help him change and learn to desire a woman. Impossible to confront his parents with such a situation. If he dared to do so, they would be in despair, seeing their family suffering instant shame, being ostracized and even cast out. Indeed, Yankl felt that, to them, the family mattered more than he did as their oldest and their only son. Impossible, impossible, impossible.

Yet not everything was negative. Yankl possessed one gift that enabled him to escape his oppressive situation: music. When Yankl was only six years old his father, his *Tatteh,* had brought home a violin for him. A wandering musician, an elderly man, had fallen sick in Rypin, and following a brief illness, had passed away. Having shown the stranger some kindness in his last days, Mendl Bradawka, Yankl's father had inherited the violin.

At first, the instrument was almost as big as the child, but Yankl struggled and persevered. He soon discovered and exploited his innate talent for music. With the help of the occasional traveling violinist who showed him some of the more intricate fingering techniques, he had become an accomplished performer. As with all other things, music, too, was set in a Jewish context. Jewish celebratory music was his specialty. At bar mitzvah parties and weddings, Yankl's playing was a favorite, accompanied by men of his father's age on the clarinet and the tsimbl or dulcimer. He was even paid for his playing, giving half to his parents, and keeping half for himself. Yankl poured all his frustrated passion into his music, closing his eyes and imagining himself accompanying a handsome young singer, male of course.

Yankl's violin became his best friend. He talked to it, polished it and communicated with it, and he could make it communicate back to him. Yankl could make his violin laugh, cry, complain and beg for more. It was a human organism to him as well as his greatest comfort in his social isolation.

He delighted in taking his instrument into the woods and performing for the trees and birds, an audience that was never dissatisfied. This became a habit every Friday afternoon, when yeshiva classes ended early in preparation for the Sabbath.

On arriving home one Wednesday evening, he greeted his parents, his *Tatteh* and his *Mommeh.* His two younger sisters, Esther and Rivka, also ran up to him as he came through the door. He was their hero. The girls had been born many years after him although their mother, Leah Bradawka, in common with many other women at that time, had given birth to two baby boys after Yankl. One had been stillborn, the other passed away shortly after his birth. Esther, the older of the two surviving girls, was six and Rivka, four. Each grasped one of Yankl's legs so that, as he strode into the room, they were lifted with each step he took, to their squealing delight.

The fragility of life made their children even more precious to Leah and Mendl Bradawka. They contemplated the young ones' playfulness with a tenderness and pleasure untainted by any fear of a possible threat to the security of their home.

"Yankl," said Tatteh, "This coming *shabbes* we'll have guests." Shabbes, the Sabbath, was the hallowed seventh day of the week, the day of rest, its strict observance being the fourth of the Ten Commandments. He continued, "My old chevrusa's son and his family are coming to stay with us on their way to Warsaw. You'll like them. They're a pleasant young couple just slightly older than you, and they have a little girl and a baby boy. They're on their way to a wedding in Warsaw."

"You should only be so happy, Yankl," Yankl's Mommeh added.

"I have plenty of time, Mommeh," Yankl responded, picturing with dread the unhappy day of his marriage.

"Just make sure you don't end up like my uncle, Aaron," she said. Aaron was Yankl's great uncle who had never married. He had left home in his twenties and emigrated to America where he made a comfortable living as a dealer in dry goods. However, he lived alone in New York.

"Don't worry about me. I'll be alright."

Following the evening meal, Yankl went to his room to practice his violin. His nimble fingers and skilful bow danced over the strings, making them sing. Yankl based the melody on a Sabbath table song, *Yoh ribbon olom,* God of the world, but he improvised, taking the tune from minor mode to major and adding musical ornaments of his own. The notes swept upward and dove downward as the boy put all his passion and prayer into the music. Downstairs, his mother sighed.

"He plays with such feeling," said Mommeh. "It seems with abnormal feeling. I can almost sense something's wrong."

Tatteh grunted. "Ach, it's nothing. Don't worry about it."

"A mother knows, Tatteh." The whole family addressed him by this name. "Something's not right. You'll see."

Chapter 2

Friday was a special day in the shtetl. As the men hurried to complete their work tasks before the onset of the holy day, the women scrambled to prepare the delicacies few of them could afford during the week. Some had already prepared the main dish, *cholent* a stew of beef, beans, egg and dumpling, carried to the baker on Friday afternoon, before the start of the Sabbath, cooked overnight in his oven, and eaten at lunchtime on the Sabbath day. Others, less well off, prepared a simple roast chicken and soup for the Friday night meal, the chicken leftovers being served cold at lunchtime the next day. Yankl's tatteh was the kosher butcher. From early morning until midday on Friday, he supplied the housewives of Rypin with chicken, tongue and beef, all sold specially for the shabbes meals.

Mommeh was a wonderful cook and baker. Her chicken soup with its hint of dill that made it uniquely delicious and her *knaidlech,* her matzah balls, were made with love. And the desserts – flans, pies, cakes – were something her entire family anticipated eagerly, from Sunday morning till Friday sundown.

As the summer sun lowered in the sky, Yankl hurried home from the study hall. He loved Fridays. If the weather was good, he would take his violin into the woods in the afternoon for his weekly performance in the midst of nature, God's creation. Then, on returning home, he would have his weekly bath in a tin tub in the kitchen, filled with heated water from the well. From there, he proceeded to the *mikve,* the ritual bath, where he immersed himself in the water in order to be ritually pure for the holy Sabbath.

This Friday, as he entered the house, he inhaled the mouth-watering aromas of the Sabbath meal, including the sweet smell of the *challahs,* the braided egg loaves that were part of the Sabbath meal ritual, and roast chicken with potatoes and vegetables, the typical menu for Friday evening.

Waiting to meet Yankl were the weekend guests. Avrum, the young husband, was in his late twenties, a handsome, strapping man with dark hair who worked as a woodsman. His wife, Eva, was on the short side and quite dumpy. She carried their two-month-old child in her arms, while their other little daughter clung to her father's hand.

"Yankl, this is Avrum, my old chevrusa's son," said Tatteh.

Avrum clasped Yankl's hand firmly.

"And this is his wife, Eva."

"I told him we should have left earlier," said Eva to nobody in particular, "but no, he had to deliver a load of wood at the last possible moment. He had to drive our trap here as if the devil himself were chasing us. I thought we'd never arrive in one piece," she complained. Eva practically ignored her introduction to Yankl. Clearly, she was not a woman to be trifled with.

Sunset was approaching. The three men left the house for the *shul,* the synagogue, where the service was held to welcome the Sabbath. The shul was the grandest building in the village, located adjacent to the study hall and towering over it. It was the only stone building in the village, its façade supported by two round columns. Inside, the cornices were decorated with painted symbols of the Jewish religion, including a *mezuzah,* the ornamental casing containing a holy text placed on doorposts; a *menora,* the six-branched candelabra reminiscent of Temple times in Jerusalem; and the palm branch with its myrtle and willow leaves and the *esrog,* a citron, the four species used symbolically at the festival of

Tabernacles. The Holy Ark containing the Torah scrolls was made of beautiful carved oak enhanced with a dark stain. Topping the ark was an artistic representation of the two tablets inscribed with the Ten Commandments. The men's section was on the ground floor while the women, who attended only on shabbes morning, and then not every shabbes morning, had their own section in the upstairs balcony, hidden from the men by a lace curtain so as not to distract them.

Yankl found the arrangement ideal. He had no interest in looking at the women, but he could survey the men on his level at his leisure, imagining that the better-looking ones were not even married.

His father sat between him and Avrum. The three men sang the melodies of the Sabbath prayers with gusto, giving thanks for coming to the end of a successful work week. At the close of the service, the men greeted each other with the traditional *Gut shabbes* before walking home to their respective families for the meal of the week.

The home ritual for the Sabbath eve proceeded as usual. The men sang *Sholom Aleichem,* a traditional melody sung on arriving home after shul on Friday evening, and as legend has it, accompanied by angels. Tatteh and Mommeh then both blessed their children, placing their hands on the head of each in turn, in order of age. Tatteh reached up to put his hands on Yankl's head. "May God make you like Ephraim and Mannaseh. May the Lord bless you and watch over you. May the Lord shine His face upon you and show you favor. May the Lord be kindly disposed toward you and grant you peace." For the girls, the parents each said: "May God make you like Sarah, Rebecca, Rachel and Leah," ending the blessing with the same words as those for Yankl. This was followed by the singing of *Ayshes chayil,* a tribute to the wife, mother and homemaker of the family.

Next came the blessing chanted over the wine at the start of the meal. Finally, after everyone had washed their hands, Mendl Bradawka, as head of the family, blessed God for providing them with bread, the two sweet egg challahs. After he had distributed a piece of the bread sprinkled with salt to everyone present, the meal itself began.

Between courses, the men sang table songs in honor of the Sabbath. Avrum had a rich baritone voice that melded well with those of Yankl and his father. They harmonized as they sang the familiar tunes, taking pleasure in their own music-making. Eva drummed her fingers on the table in accompaniment. By religious convention, she was forbidden to join the men in song for fear that the men might become sexually distracted by the voice of a woman. However, quite obviously this was a situation that frustrated her, and as the men began the fourth table song, she began to hum along tunelessly. Yankl exchanged glances with his frowning father, but Avrum seemed oblivious to his wife's breach of etiquette. Worse was yet to come.

Following dessert, Tatteh asked Yankl to lead the grace after meals. Yankl's sweet voice began the opening anthem, *Shir hama'alos,* joined by the men. Mommeh sat silent while Eva, taking advantage of a situation where nobody had taken the initiative to hush her, hummed more loudly. But singing in unison was something quite beyond her capacities. The sound emanating from her throat was raucous and, to varying degrees, out of tune.

Nothing could have had a more disastrous effect on Yankl who was leading the prayer. Somebody singing out of tune without being aware of it provoked an uncontrollable desire in him to laugh. And this was a woman's voice, a phenomenon with which he was totally unfamiliar. As he intoned the introductory verses for the men alone, he could feel the panic rising. If Eva continued to sing as the grace continued, he knew that he would be unable to control himself. His father shot him a warning glance across the table and slowly shook his head, knowing what might happen.

As the singing continued, Eva's humming seemed to grow louder. She scratched her head, slightly tilting her *shaytel,* the wig worn by married women out of modesty. She looked and sounded quite ridiculous. Yankl tried to look away. He thought of his own personal tragedy. It did not help. He thought of his poor *Booba,* his father's mother, who had died the year before, and with whom he had felt so close. That did not help either. He thought of death but not even that helped. As he led the prayers, he felt his cheekbones freeze, his eyes ached, his chest heaved.

He stopped singing, stifling a giggle. The blood rushed from the soles of his feet to the roots of his hair like an accelerated sunrise. His hand went to his mouth. The company fell silent. "Excuse me," he muttered as he jumped up from the table and ran through the house and into the small backyard. He collapsed on a bench in a paroxysm of laughter, holding his sides, totally helpless. He felt so ashamed as his hysteria brought him to tears, but not even that could stop his peals of laughter. One or two neighbors came out of their houses to investigate the cause of the uncontrolled amusement, only to hear Yankl gasp, between the gales of merriment, "It's alright. I'm sorry, I'm sorry…"

Back in the dining room, his father took over leading the grace after meals, apologizing for his son's rude behavior. He, his family and the guests concluded the prayer and the women rose from the table to clear away what was left of the meal. Tatteh and Avrum remained at the table, each with a glass of lemon tea.

"Does this happen often?" asked Avrum. "Would you like me to go and talk to him?"

"Please do," responded Tatteh. "Perhaps you can drive some sense into his head. Sometimes he can be so immature. See what you can do, and I thank you."

Avrum left Mendl pensive at the table and walked through the house and into the backyard. The full moon shone on Yankl who, by then, had recovered his composure. The harmonies of neighboring families singing table songs in honor of the Sabbath filled the air.

"I'm sorry, Avrum," Yankl said. "There are times when I completely lose control and things get out of hand. I can't help it."

Avrum sat on the bench next to Yankl. "I have a wonderful wife, Yankl, but unfortunately, she doesn't realize the effect her singing can have on people. And it's not an effect that makes me either proud or envious." He smiled. Yankl noticed the whiteness of his teeth. "Come, let's take a walk together. You can tell me a little about yourself and you'll feel better."

They stood and walked to a gate in the fence at the back of the yard leading to an alley that ran between the houses. Avrum and Yankl went into the alley, walking slowly, their shadows preceding them in the moonlight. They made small talk, Avrum telling Yankl about his work, cutting wood, making planks and even doing a little carpentry. Yankl told Avrum about his life in the yeshiva, and his passion for music and the violin.

"I sometimes play music at weddings," he said. "Whose wedding are you going to in Warsaw?"

"It's my first cousin's, on my father's side. There's nothing quite like our weddings, as you know Yankl. And I wouldn't miss it for the world!"

There was a silence. Suddenly, Yankl blurted out: "I don't ever want to get married. Marriage is not for everyone."

"But you must, Yankl. Everyone marries and everyone expects it of you. A handsome young man like you. Any girl would be honored."

Yankl did not respond. "What shall I do?" he mumbled, almost to himself.

"Listen, Yankl," Avrum said. "With your great future in music and your good looks, you'll see. Everything will work out."

Yankl felt the firm grip of the older man's arm around his shoulders. It seemed to him as if a flash of lightning passed between Avrum's hand and his own arm. "I'm not so sure. I wish I could find someone who understands me," he said. "It's difficult to find someone to talk to."

The two men were approaching a large tree. The trunk emerged from a backyard, but the leafy branches overhung the alley, casting a deep shadow. Avrum stopped. He turned Yankl to face him and took his face between his hands. "You're a fine boy, Yankl, and you'll make a fine man," he whispered, and his lips gently brushed the tip of Yankl's nose. Yankl's hands went haltingly to Avrum's arms and held them. Avrum took Yankl in his arms and gently drew their bodies together. Yankl felt the hardness of his father's guest against his own rising excitement.

"It's alright," said Avrum in Yankl's ear. "It's alright to feel this way." His hand dropped to Yankl's aroused member. Yankl was in a dreamlike state. He heard a loud hissing in his head like a snake poised to strike, but he knew he could not draw back now. The two men exposed themselves, and gripping each other in a strong embrace, they quickly erupted in a violent ejaculation. Yankl reeled backward from the effect of the physical release and all his pent up emotion. Avrum put his arm around him to steady him. "Shh," he whispered. "Everything is as it should be..."

It took Yankl a few minutes to collect himself. As he adjusted his clothing, he had a flashback to the weeks before his bar mitzvah, when Tatteh had explained the facts of life to him. His father had been so matter-of-fact about it. But what Yankl remembered most was his father's emphasis on the sanctity of sex within marriage. The holiness of the act. So was this what he wanted? Sex with a married man in a back alley? With a man bound by holy matrimony to his wife?

He turned to face Avrum. "But how can you make love with me and love your wife?" he asked, naively.

Avrum pondered the question. "Well," he said hesitantly, "I do love my wife."

Yankl felt hot tears stinging his eyes. He felt betrayed, as isolated as ever. Yet what did he expect? What right had he to expect anything? This was to be his destiny. Furtive sex, condemned by the Torah as a forbidden act, 'an abomination'. It was all so clear and so completely unfair. To have been given everything in life – loving parents, a comfortable home, friends, family, music, a secure future – and ultimately to have nothing. He had no more to say to Avrum, but pride prevented him from giving way to the tears of frustration and anger that brimmed up in his eyes.

They walked back slowly to the house, each returning to his own world. When they arrived, the house was silent, everyone having retired for the night.

"Go to bed, Yankl," said Avrum. "And let's forget about this."

Once in his room, Yankl lay on his bed, looking at the waning moon through the window. There was nothing and nobody to look forward to. But, at least, he knew the desires he felt were not only his own.

Over shabbes, Yankl had no opportunity to speak with Avrum alone. Indeed, Avrum seemed to avoid him, as if he were ashamed of what had occurred between them. Yankl observed Avrum at the shabbes lunchtime meal, passing dishes to Eva, his wife, with great solicitousness, almost fawning over her, as if to prove to Yankl that their nighttime encounter had been no more than a passing fancy and meant absolutely nothing. Yankl felt disgusted. His conversation with Avrum had obviously been Avrum's ploy to obtain no more than his own physical release.

Nevertheless, on reflection as he rested later in the day, Yankl realized that the incident with Avrum was entirely natural for him. It was what he had yearned for ever since puberty. He could no more think of it as a sin, an 'abomination', than the act of eating or any other bodily function. The thought of having relations with a woman, on the other hand, seemed as unnatural to him as doing so with a household pet. Yet he felt no hostility toward women on a day-to-day basis, not that he had any connection with them apart from his Mommeh and his sisters. In the shtetl, even social contact with members of the opposite sex was forbidden outside marriage. Yankl considered the prohibition quite artificial: half of the human race was beyond his range of experience. What an odd, even unnatural situation!

Avrum and his family left on the Sunday. After thanking the Bradawkas for their hospitality, Avrum turned to Yankl. "I look forward to dancing at your wedding, Yankl," was his final comment. It took all Yankl's effort to prevent himself from sneering.

"Did you ever see Avrum again?" I interjected.

"No, nor did I want to. I felt used by him. Abused by him. The experience also made me realize that attraction to one or the other sex sometimes comes in shades of grey. While I never felt any physical desire for women, Avrum was clearly capable of being aroused by both women and men. It is something I cannot understand."

"And I fail to understand it, too. But it's a fact of life that I accept, although I don't believe it happens often. And it can be the cause of greater pain to others, as you yourself discovered."

"I only hope that Eva never learned of that particular aspect of her husband's character. It would have destroyed her," said Yankl.

Chapter 3

Having had his first physical experience with a man, Yankl felt trapped. He needed not only physical relief, but an emotional outlet. His daily routine became oppressive and he felt that he was inevitably destined for tragedy. Once again, the urge arose in him to confide in someone, to share his pain. And Eliyohu was the obvious choice.

One Friday, when the study hall closed at noon in preparation for shabbes, Yankl steeled himself to speak to Eliyohu.

"Could we, perhaps, take a walk and talk after our study session? I have something I want to discuss with you." Eliyohu nodded his consent.

The morning seemed unnaturally long to Yankl. He tried to concentrate on reading from the convoluted text that had been assigned, his mind constantly wandering to what he would say to Eliyohu. Could he trust him? How would he react? Would he just listen, or would he be disgusted? Finally, the studying came to end. The students greeted each other with *Gut shabbes* and, at leisure, wandered off to their homes.

Eliyohu and Yankl walked to the edge of the shtetl and sat on a low wall enclosing a yard. Inside, on the patch of grass, some young children, freed from their own heavy study schedule, were finally able to give vent to their childish impulses by playing a game of tag.

"What do you want to talk about, Yankl?" asked Eliyohu.

Yankl was silent for a few moments. "Give me a minute. This is not easy for me." He took a deep breath. "Eliyohu, what

I have to say to you must remain between us. I want you to take my hand and swear to me that it will never go further."

Eliyohu looked into the distance. "Are you sure you want to talk to me about this?"

"Yes," said Yankl. "I really need to talk to someone and you're the only person I can think of. So, please give me your hand… and your promise."

Almost reluctantly, with a feeling of foreboding, Eliyohu held out his hand, which Yankl seized and gripped. "Thank you," he said. "You don't know how much this means to me."

"Well?" said Eliyohu, as Yankl paused once again.

"Do you have feelings for women, Eliyohu?"

"Yes, of course I do. In fact, next week, my Tatteh has arranged for me to meet a girl who will probably become my wife. She comes from a good family, and I'm told she's not bad looking."

"Is that what you want?"

"Of course. What else would I want?" said Eliyohu, almost brusquely.

"Well," Yankl took a deep breath, "It's not what I want for myself." Eliyohu looked startled.

"But everyone wants to get married and have a family. It's only natural."

"Yes," Yankl hesitated, "but it's not natural for me."

"What do you mean?" asked Eliyohu, as his thoughts tried to avoid what he expected would come.

"I'm not attracted to women, physically I mean."

"Oh," said Eliyohu. "Then what?"

"I can't help it, but I have feelings for men," said Yankl.

Eliyohu stood up. "You can't. You mustn't. It's a sin. It's an abomination. It says so in the Torah."

"But I do," Yankl protested. "It's not something I chose. It's not something I would choose. It's just the way I am. What can I do?" All the despair Yankl had felt in the past suddenly surfaced as he covered his face with his hands and rocked backward and forward as he did in the study hall, but now out of hopelessness. "What can I do?" he repeated.

"I don't know," said Eliyohu. "Change. Try and force yourself to like a woman. To love a woman and have children. Otherwise what will become of you? You will end up alone, with nobody to take care of you in your old age. No children, no grandchildren. People will avoid you. Yankl, you must try and change," pleaded Eliyohu.

"Could *you* change, Eliyohu? Yes, you. What if the world were different. What if men married men? Could you force yourself to marry a man?"

"But it isn't and I couldn't," said Eliyohu. "This is the way things are and you must adapt to them."

"I can't," said Yankl with a sense of finality. "I just want to be what I am."

"Yankl, you are my friend. But a Jew cannot stand by and let another Jew harm himself. For your own good, for the sake of your future happiness, I beg of you, try and change."

"Eliyohu, if I marry, I will cause only unhappiness to my wife and family. I cannot lie with a woman."

"Then I'm sorry for you," said Eliyohu, turning away. "Look, I promised I'd keep your secret, and I will. But I cannot approve of you with a clear conscience. This is the way of the world, and if things are not as they should be, it is our job to put them right – *tikkun olam.* Try to understand."

Yankl felt he was being patronized. For how long had he himself tried to understand? Nothing made any sense. This is the way God had created him, and although he would have given anything to change, he could not. This was the way of *his* world.

With resignation, he said: "Eliyohu, I do understand. Thank you for listening to me. I'm at least happy that someone knows how I feel, even if you don't sympathize. I am happy that you are going to get married, and I will share your happiness. But perhaps you should forget this conversation. I will deal with my situation as best I can, with God's help. I'm going home now, and I wish you a *Gut shabbes.*" He stood up. Their conversation had been useless.

They shook hands. Yankl's conversation with Eliyohu would remain as secret as the incident with Avrum. Both had been fruitless episodes, with no past and no future. Yankl walked through the village to his parents' house, where he took his violin and went back out into the woods. As his bow slid over the strings, he felt his familiar sense of isolation smother him like an evil cloud. Then, in spite of his best efforts, the tears started coursing down his cheeks.

A few weeks later, Eliyohu was married. As usual, the ceremony was simple and beautiful. Eliyohu looked very handsome under the *chuppah,* the wedding canopy. For the ceremony, he donned a white smock, a *kittel,* which he wore over black pants and a white shirt, a sign of spiritual purity. His bride walked slowly down the aisle in the synagogue on her father's arm. She was dressed in a straight-cut white dress, her head concealed under a white veil, and a bouquet of daisies in her hands. Leaving her father standing under the chuppah, she walked around her groom seven times, as is the custom. A specially gifted cantor had been brought to Rypin from Warsaw for the occasion, and his rich melodious baritone added color to the ceremony. As the bride's mother lifted the veil for her daughter to drink wine from the silver wine cup, then shared by her groom, Yankl was surprised to see how plain the bride was. Such a handsome groom, he thought, with such an ordinary-looking bride. She must have a beautiful soul, he thought, smiling to himself. The ceremony ended with Eliyohu crushing a glass underfoot. This part of the ceremony is a sign of mourning for the destruction of the two holy Temples in Jerusalem. No joy can be complete in Judaism without the rebuilding of the Temple. As the goblet shattered, all present shouted *"Mazel tov!"* for good luck.

The wedding party and guests then adjourned to the study hall for the festivities. It had been cleared of the usual desks and chairs and converted for the occasion into a reception hall.

Sumptuous food was laid out on the tables, prepared by the local housewives. The men and women sat in different sections, separated by a thick curtain. Only the musical group, of which Yankl was a member, was visible to both men and women and, after the meal, which was followed by grace, men and women danced in segregated sections of the room to the traditional wedding music. Men never danced with the women; even here, there was very little social contact between the two sexes.

Yankl played his violin with gusto. He tried to imagine his own wedding. How romantic it would be! And then he imagined his wedding night. Instinctively, he tried to blot out the thought, running the bow over the strings with even more zeal.

Once married, Eliyohu could no longer be Yankl's chevrusa. First, he had to earn a living to support his new wife and the children that were bound to come, so he apprenticed with his father part-time, learning the trade of shoemaker. And then, when he attended the study hall, he sat in the *kollel* section, a room set aside for students who were married. Inevitably, he and Yankl drifted apart.

"And did you miss him?" I asked. "I have always found it so difficult to let a relationship go, especially when there is such a strongly shared past."

Yankl answered: "When Eliyohu was so inflexible with me, I immediately felt a distance grow between us. Our past meant nothing to him. He could never accept me for what I was, for my true nature. I would always have been obliged to play a part when I was with him. His marriage just sealed the end to our friendship. Otherwise, it would have drifted away slowly. In a way I was relieved not to have to deal with him every day and pretend that everything was as it should be."

"Thank God, attitudes where I live have changed. I no longer have to hide and be ashamed of the way I feel."

"And where do you live?"

"I live in Canada. It's the country north of the United States of America, almost as big as Russia and just as cold. But if I were to tell my best friend what you told Eliyohu, and if he were an educated person, he would probably shrug his shoulders and say 'So what!'"

"But what does that mean?" asked Yankl.

"It means that today, in Canada, people who love others of the same sex are generally not treated as outcasts or sick. In fact, they can actually marry."

"Marry?" Yankl was astonished.

"Yes, marry. Two men or two women can marry."

Yankl laughed. "But that's absurd! How can two men or two women marry?"

"It's not so absurd. You, yourself, when you made your confession to Eliyohu, asked 'What if men married men?' Well, here they can. The ceremony is usually non-religious, although some clergy, mainly non-Jewish do officiate at ceremonies for gentiles. The marriage is what we call a civil marriage, one with all the legal rights as in a contract, but without any religious content."

"So people like you and me are like everyone else?"

"Yes, in the eyes of the law. But of course, it will take time for everyone to accept this. They have to overcome centuries of prejudice inherited from past generations. But once they see that our values are not so different from theirs, they'll understand."

"It's something I have difficulty in understanding, too," said Yankl.

"How could it be otherwise?" I said.

Chapter 4

Shmulik Belman was round. Everything about him was round, from his face to his body to his arms and legs. At rest, even his little mouth was round although he often stretched his lips in a smile or gave one of his frequent little giggles, revealing his white teeth, also round. Shmulik had an engaging character, always wishing to be of service to others.

Perhaps it was because he suffered from a feeling of inferiority that he sought general approval, which he won easily, although few of the yeshiva boys sought him out either as a chevrusa or as a confidant. They considered him, with his almost constant smile, to be slightly simple, and his knowledge of Talmud was far from profound. His arguments on the texts were always facile and unsupported by relevant sources.

Rabbi Levy, the head of the yeshiva, assigned Shmulik the task of setting out the volumes on the study tables and putting them back on the bookshelves when the yeshiva boys had finished with them at the end of the day. For this, Shmulik received a small stipend. He came from one of the poorer families in Rypin and the rabbi wished to give his family some support in his own small way. Shmulik's father, Dov Belman, was a carter, delivering goods, foodstuffs and materials to the general store in the shtetl, and transporting people to nearby villages where they could pick up the stage to travel farther afield.

Dov Belman and his wife, Tzeitel, had four daughters as well as Shmulik, their only son and the oldest child in the family. By some miracle, they had managed to find a match for him since he was neither physically attractive nor endowed with any skill that would render him capable of supporting a wife and family. Yet from the day when his betrothal had been announced in July to the approaching wedding day in August, Shmulik's smile had faded and was rarely seen on his usually jovial face.

One Tuesday morning in the dog days of early August, Shmulik was nowhere to be seen in the yeshiva. Another boy distributed the volumes of Talmud, everyone believing that Shmulik was unwell or that the humidity of the previous night had left him exhausted. The morning began as usual with the boys settling down to their day of study when a male passerby entered the study hall asking for the rabbi.

"Mrs. Belman is outside," he said to one of the boys. "She wants to speak to the rabbi urgently."

Rabbi Levy came to the large double doors at the entrance of the study hall. He saw Mrs. Belman, a short, stout woman, with an anxious look on her face.

"What's the matter, Mrs. Belman? How is Shmulik?" he asked.

"Rabbi Levy, is he not inside? I'm very worried. He didn't come home last night." Mrs. Belman had difficulty coping with life. With four young daughters, her husband and Shmulik to take care of and feed, and with little money to buy the household necessities, every day was a struggle to survive.

"You'd better come in," said the rabbi, not happy to have been distracted from his teaching duties. "Let's go into my study."

Mrs. Belman sat in the guest chair facing the rabbi across his wide desk. In her hand was a kerchief that she twisted ceaselessly in her anxiety.

"Where can he be?" she said. "He hasn't been himself in the last few weeks, moody, and snapping at the girls. Rabbi, I'm so worried. He should be so happy that we found a wife for him."

"Come, now, Mrs. Belman. Let's not allow things to get out of proportion. Perhaps he was in a deep discussion with a friend and spent the night with his friend's family."

"Rabbi, you know that's not my Shmulik. He gets along with all the boys but he has no close friendship with any of them."

"But it is a possibility. Wait for me here. I'll go into the study hall and ask if any of the students have seen him."

The rabbi left Mrs. Belman in his study. She was visibly shaken at the thought of all the possibilities – an accident, perhaps an attack by anti-Semitic youth out for blood at the edge of the shtetl. Such things had been known to happen.

Rabbi Levy marched into the study hall, clapping his hands loudly to attract the boys' attention. Their singsong as they studied died down as all the students looked at him expectantly.

"Has anyone seen Shmulik?" he shouted. The boys shook their heads and looked at each other. "Are you sure?" Silence.

The rabbi stood at the edge of the hall uncertain as to what to do. He could not ignore Mrs. Belman's suspicions especially since he, too, had noticed the change in Shmulik's demeanor, putting it down to nerves. He walked back to his study, the boys' droning starting up again as they went back to their books.

"Mrs. Belman, no news," he said. "What can I do?"

"We must look for him, and look for him now, rabbi. Perhaps he's had an accident. He may have been attacked by wild animals in the woods or fallen somewhere and can't move."

Reluctantly, the rabbi agreed. A day of study might be lost, but a life could be saved. He marched back to the study hall.

"Gentlemen," he said formally. "Shmulik may have had an accident or lost his way in the forest. So close your books now and we'll go and look for him. Those of you to my left will go through the shtetl and ask whether anyone has seen him.

Ask people in the street. Knock on every door. Those of you to my right will come with me and we will look for him in the forest."

The students left their places and went outside. Mrs. Belman stood at the exit to the yeshiva, leaning against the doorpost. "Please, please find him, safe and sound," she said almost to herself. She raised her hand to the *mezuzah* on the doorpost, that small ornate case containing a parchment with Judaism's holiest prayer, and touched her fingers to her lips.

The woman's obvious distress affected the boys and stirred their motivation. They all liked Shmulik in an impersonal way and would not have wanted him to come to any harm. The two groups set out in different directions, one to question the villagers, another to search the forest, frequently calling his name. Yankl joined the group searching in the woods.

The heat and humidity of the day added to the boys' discomfort and anxiety. The group that remained in the shtetl asked everyone in the street if they had seen Shmulik. They knocked on doors, always receiving the same negative answer. The group in the forest fanned out, calling Shmulik's name as they advanced deeper into the trees.

Yankl had a passing acquaintance with Shmulik. On one occasion, shortly after his betrothal, Shmulik had even asked to speak to him confidentially. For days, Shmulik had hovered near Yankl's desk in the study hall, seeming to want to speak to him. Finally, Yankl had said to him: "Shmulik, can I help you with anything? Is there something you want?"

"No, no. There's nothing. Nothing," came the reply as Shmulik hurried away, placing the books he was carrying on the tables. It had taken days for Shmulik to raise the courage to even approach Yankl. Shmulik had never given much thought to his own sexuality until faced with the prospect of marriage. Then, as he envisaged the physical implications of wedlock, a sense of revulsion had overtaken him. He just could not do it.

He felt like a fox surrounded by yelping hounds. Perhaps talking about it would help.

Shmulik had no more than a feeling about Yankl and the aura of empathy that he exuded. But how could he broach such a delicate subject? Fear of rejection and ridicule gripped him. But fear of marriage tipped the balance in favor of speaking to Yankl. He had to do something, anything to face his dilemma.

A few days later, Yankl looked up from the text he was studying to find Shmulik standing in front of him.

"Yes. Yes, there was something. There is something I want to talk to you about," Shmulik blurted out, his face flushed.

"Well then, let's meet after *ma'ariv,* the evening prayer, and we can talk about it."

But at the arranged time, Yankl waited in vain. Shmulik's apprehension about Yankl's reaction had proved stronger than his dread at the thought of marriage. He made a hasty escape from the study hall after the evening prayer. When he failed to appear, Yankl, half suspecting that Shmulik had more in common with him than he cared to admit, did not pursue the matter, nor did he take the opportunity to do so in the next few days. He felt absolutely no rapport with Shmulik although, had Shmulik confided in him, Yankl would not have hesitated to listen to him and offer moral support.

As the boys wandered through the woods calling Shmulik's name from time to time, Yankl hoped and prayed that Shmulik had done nothing to harm himself. If, indeed, his *yetzer hora,* his evil inclination or, in this case, his sexual drive, was the same as Yankl's, Shmulik, with the looming prospect of marriage, may have seen no escape and decided on the ultimate solution.

Slowly the boys walked forward, calling and looking around for any sign of life. For an hour and a half they searched in vain. Then a shout went up.

"Over there." It was one of the boys on the extreme left of the line of searchers. "Up there," he cried again. *"Oy gevalt!"*

Everyone looked up. Hanging by a rope round his neck from the limb of a large tree, its trunk inclined, was Shmulik's lifeless body. The group gathered around the tree as Rabbi Levy hurried over.

"Does anyone have a knife?" he shouted. "We must cut him down." One of the boys always carried a pocket knife after having been attacked by a street gang, long ago. He climbed up the sloping tree trunk to the branch from which Shmulik had hanged himself, and as the rabbi held Shmulik's body, he severed the rope Shmulik had used as a noose. His body was a dead weight and Rabbi Levy asked the boys nearest him for help in lowering it to the ground.

They laid him in the undergrowth at the foot of the tree. Pinned to Shmulik's shirt was a note, visible to the rabbi and to all his former classmates gathered around.

It read:

> *Forgive me. Marriage would have been an even greater sin.*

The older boys looked at each other. The note was somewhat of an enigma. How could marriage be a sin? Would it have been a sin for Shmulik in particular? And if marriage were a sin, what could possibly be the lesser sin mentioned in his note? Slowly the light dawned on them. Shmulik had been quite depressed of late instead of reveling in the joy of his forthcoming wedding. Perhaps he was not looking forward to it, even dreading it. They recalled his simple, almost silly smile. Recently, it had faded, then vanished. Perhaps he was not attracted to women at all and the lesser sin could have been an attraction to men. Could that have been his sin?

Meanwhile, the younger boys were staring at Shmulik's prone, motionless body, laid out on the grass. One or two of the younger boys who had barely reached the age of bar mitzvah started to cry. The rabbi quickly muttered the blessing to be recited when faced with death: Blessed are you, Lord our God, King of the universe, the true Judge. He then took control.

"Help them. Comfort them," he said, addressing some of the older boys who put their arms around the shoulders of the youngsters in distress, still children at heart.

"Yankl, Eliyohu, Mendl and Sender, carry the boy back. But let me go ahead and prepare Mrs. Belman. And may the Holy One Blessed be He give us all strength."

Rabbi Levy hurried off as the four young men gently lifted the stiff corpse onto their shoulders to take it back to the shtetl. Yankl was consumed with guilt. Perhaps, had he taken the initiative with Shmulik, he could have helped to avert this tragedy. Life, the highest value in Judaism, had been destroyed, in itself a sin. Now the family could not even sit *shiva,* pass a week of mourning with visits from friends and family. As for Shmulik, his body would be buried at the edge of the cemetery, an outcast. Tears welled up in Yankl's eyes. This body, whose weight he was bearing, could so easily have been his own.

Never, he told himself, never can things get so bad that I will take my own life. Whatever fate lies ahead of me, I vow that I will live out my life. It is too precious a thing to surrender to the will of others. I will not let them do this terrible thing to me.

That night, the humid weather broke with a thunderous storm that prevented anyone in the shtetl from enjoying a restful sleep. Yankl drifted in and out of wakefulness, seeing Shmulik's smiling face before his eyes, and then his more recent look of despair.

Early the next morning, the humidity had cleared and a dank mist rose from the sodden earth toward a watery sun. Rabbi Levy and Shmulik's father followed four of the yeshiva boys, Yankl being one of them, bearing Shmulik's body on a wide plank. He was wrapped in his *tallis,* his prayer shawl, and covered with a sheet used as a shroud. They trudged through the cemetery, past the other graves to an empty space near the fence.

There, the grave having been dug overnight, Shmulik was buried in the presence of his father, the rabbi and the four boys, their number insufficient for a *minyan,* the quorum of men required for Dov Belman to recite the *Kaddish* for his deceased son, the mourner's prayer for the dead. Nevertheless, Rabbi Levy intoned the *El molleh rachamim,* God full of mercy, the community prayer for the occasion. As Dov Belman turned away from the grave, his eyes streaming with tears, he said in a low voice: "He was a good boy. A really good boy," the only eulogy that Shmulik, his only son, would be allowed.

For weeks following the tragedy, the boys and young men in the yeshiva still expected Shmulik to appear to distribute and collect their books, without hope. They missed his simple smile and his silly giggle and mourned him in their own way. As for Yankl, he finally came to terms with his own lack of response to Shmulik's shy approach. It had been Shmulik's decision to end his life and whatever advice Yankl may have given him might not have saved him. Yankl did not even know how he himself would have reacted, faced with a similar situation, one that he realized was a distinct possibility in the future.

"When I think of Shmulik, I remember how helpless I felt. I was unwilling to seek a solution to his problem, perhaps because I had a premonition that, one day, I would have to face exactly the same predicament."

"Yet," I said, "you were so aware of your own isolation. Don't you think that just by encouraging Shmulik to talk to you, you could have given him some comfort? A problem shared is so much easier to bear."

"Look," said Yankl, defensively, "we are all guilty of not acting as we should in some circumstances, either by doing something or not doing it. Of course, I feel guilty for not having responded to his

approach. But I never thought for a moment that he would take his own life. I didn't think that he would be brave enough. But he was."

Chapter 5

The months passed. Yankl studied with a series of chevrusas. Some left to get married while others came from families who later decided to move away or emigrate. With none of them could he establish the rapport he had felt with Eliyohu, with whom he had grown up. He studied with his new chevrusas but had little social contact with them beyond the study hall. Their social life was contained within their immediate families and, at most, within their extended families.

One spring day, when Yankl was nineteen, he arrived at the study hall to find a new chevrusa, sitting opposite him. Velvel Gambiner was a young man of eighteen who had recently moved to Rypin with his family. His grandfather had been the shtetl baker, but when he grew too old to perform the heavy work involved in running the bakery, Velvel's father, also a baker, had moved back with his family to take over the business and keep the shtetl supplied with bread. Velvel's older brother already worked with his father in the bakery and would soon marry a distant cousin. His younger brother still attended the cheder. Velvel's mother made her contribution to the business by baking delicious cookies that many a local housewife passed off as her own. Velvel was the middle son of three; there were no daughters in the family.

In appearance, Velvel was slightly shorter than Yankl and his most distinguishing feature was a mop of irrepressible, curly, red hair. Velvel had smiling eyes set in a strong, square face, and he was blessed with a curious mind. He lived in the same neighborhood as Yankl, so they would walk home together after the day of study, extending their discussion, and even venturing into some talk of life outside the study hall.

Yankl shared his joy of music with Velvel, who in turn, showed great interest in hearing Yankl play his violin. "Will you play it for me?" he asked. "I could go with you into the woods on one of your Friday afternoons, and you could give me my very own private concert."

Yankl felt flattered. He knew people enjoyed hearing him play at weddings and bar mitzvah parties, but there had never been anyone who had expressed a desire to hear him play solo just for the sheer pleasure of it. He had always felt like an appendage to other people's happy events, never an event in himself. So some weeks later on a Friday afternoon, after Yankl picked up his violin from home, Velvel accompanied him into the woods.

They walked deep into the forest, the afternoon sun casting shimmering patches of light on the shaded grassy undergrowth. Conversation between the two young men seemed to fade to silence. Yankl admitted to himself that he was nervous. He had never played to an audience of one. Velvel, for his part, was nervous, too, but for another reason.

Velvel had never experienced any physical desire for either men or women, and he just accepted this as natural. In time, he told himself, I'll be introduced to a woman who will become my wife. She will be able to arouse me and we'll have children. Yet, in the month or so that he had studied with Yankl and grown to know him on a personal level, he had felt more than a shared interest in Talmud. When he looked at Yankl's dark face and brooding eyes, he had felt something that, he hated to admit, approached passion. He sensed that Yankl was deeply unhappy and, more than anything else, Velvel wanted to comfort him. He wanted to hold Yankl and tell him that he had his support for whatever was troubling him. He wanted to explain to Yankl that he could rely on him as a confidant who wanted only to help him find happiness. Finally, it dawned upon him: he loved Yankl!

The rustling of their footsteps plowing through the undergrowth covered their silence as they reached a glade with a large oak tree and short grass growing round the base of its thick trunk.

"Here," announced Yankl. "I'll give you your concert here."

As Yankl took his violin from its case, Velvel sat on the ground, his back to the tree. Yankl tuned his instrument, then closing his eyes, he began a sad, sentimental melody, well known to all the Jews in the shtetl, entitled *Belz, Mein Shtetle Belz,* about the shtetl of Belz. The notes soared up to the treetops blending with the melody of the birdsong.

Velvel was enchanted. As the final phrase of the performance faded, He said, "Yankl, that was beautiful. Play some more for me."

Wishing to change the mood for something slightly more cheerful, Yankl chose a popular *bulgar,* a dance tune. The melody started slowly but gradually became faster, ending with a great flourish. Again, Yankl closed his eyes. As the tune quickened, Velvel rose to his feet and started dancing, his feet stepping and stamping in time to the music and his arms stretched above his head, fingers snapping to the beat. As the music finished, Yankl opened his eyes to see Velvel standing, his arms held high and his breath coming in short gasps.

"Yankl, play it again and dance with me!" Yankl felt no compunction about dancing with Velvel; after all, men danced with men all the time at communal celebrations. So he recommenced the famous folksong. This time, his eyes were open staring intensely into Velvel's. Velvel sang in accompaniment to Yankl's music. As the rhythm picked up speed, Yankl kept in step with him. Faster and faster they danced, circling each other and panting with the effort. At the final flourish, Yankl laughed with the sheer joy of the moment, leaned back against the tree and held his violin and bow outstretched in a dramatic gesture. Suddenly, Velvel was there in his arms, their breathless bodies leaning together as they fought to regain their wind. Without a second thought, Yankl lowered his arms, embracing Velvel, his cheek luxuriating at the touch of Velvel's mass of red curls. There they stood frozen in the moment.

Velvel drew his head back, looked into Yankl's eyes and gently kissed him, mouth to mouth. Taken aback, Yankl's first instinct was to turn away, until he suddenly realized that this was precisely what he wanted – the most normal thing to happen in the world. He returned Velvel's kiss. Each felt the other's arousal. Yankl placed his violin and bow on the ground. Then they slowly undressed each other. Velvel's chest was coated with a layer of soft ginger hair, like a furry forest animal, while Yankl's body was mostly smooth. Without a word being spoken, they lay down together in the bed of green undergrowth and made passionate love.

As their breathing returned to normal, they continued to lie together, wondering at the beauty of the experience. Each, with eyes shut, passed a hand over the other's face, like a blind man reading Braille, their hands trying to commit to memory the other's facial features before their narrative continued. And yet the intrusive conventions of the world they lived in could not be ignored.

"Was that wrong?" said Velvel. "Have we sinned?"

Yankl stroked Velvel's hair. "Shh. How can it be wrong? I have yearned for this moment for a long, long time. The Holy One, blessed be He, created us this way. And God gave us the ability to love. Could God be wrong?"

"But people think it's wrong. What would they say?"

"They'll never know. It will be between you, me and God."

"Yankl, I think I love you. Is that possible? Love between two men?"

"Of course, it's possible. It's even in the *T'nach*, the Bible. I don't believe David and Jonathan were just friends in spite of what they tell us. David loved Jonathan with a 'love exceeding that of a woman', and Jonathan 'delighted in David'. There was more than friendship there."

"But people don't understand. They won't want to understand."

"Velvel," said Yankl. "We have done nobody any harm. Nobody has seen us. Let what has happened be our secret. It will be that much more precious."

As they strolled back through the forest, Yankl could hear the music in his heart. At last, he was no longer alone. At last, there was someone like him. And at last, there was someone who liked him – even loved him. And when he thought again about Velvel, Yankl experienced that inner stirring in the pit of his stomach and in his head that told him that he wanted to spoil Velvel – he did not know how – and to protect him. He desired him, physically, too. Perhaps he loved Velvel, too.

"Will we do this again?" he asked Velvel.

"If you want to as much as I do, of course we will. Next Friday?"

"Next Friday."

As Yankl entered the shabbes house, his face glowed. Delicious aromas emanated from the range as Mommeh made the final preparations for the shabbes meal, fussing around in the kitchen and asking her two little daughters to fetch this and that.

"Where have you been?" Mommeh asked Yankl.

"Just playing my violin in the forest."

"You look different. Does shabbes make you so happy?"

"I composed a new *niggun*, a melody without words, in the forest, and I'm quite pleased with it."

The shabbes meal proceeded as usual, with good food, singing and blessings. Yankl ached to be alone with his thoughts, and as night closed in, he lay down thankfully on his bed. How his world had changed in twenty-four short hours! This time yesterday, he was still consumed by his own lonely tragedy. Now he knew someone else was thinking of him, just as he was thinking of Velvel. Fate, he thought, had finally smiled upon him. No, not fate; God had answered his prayer for which he thanked Him. But would it last? Could this be a permanent solution? Could two male lovers, surrounded as they were by a society that denied their feelings and their very existence, form a strong relationship? They would have to take great care not to be discovered. No adoring looks, no secret code words, and of course, never any touching in public.

The Sabbath passed, and on the first day of the week, Yankl and Velvel found themselves once again facing each other across a desk in the study hall. They were both shyly embarrassed, not knowing quite what to say to each other. They both leafed through the heavy tomes of their Talmud.

"Shall we begin?" Yankl suggested. They found the passage selected for reading and discussion that day.

Velvel began. "Rav said… that Yankl has beautiful eyes." Yankl looked up sharply, surprised, and smiled before he continued the supposed reading.

"Rava said… Yankl loves Velvel. But…"

"But what?" asked Velvel, alarmed.

"Rava also said: we have to be very careful. Everyone thinks that what we're doing and what we're feeling is a sin. But we know how we feel. So let us play the game. Let's pretend nothing has happened. Let's pretend we're just chevrusas, as before. We must do nothing to arouse suspicion. Let's study, Velvel, until Friday."

Strangely, studying the complicated texts flowed more smoothly. Everything seemed as clear as unquestioning faith. Meanings fell into place like an easy jigsaw puzzle. For the two young men, the world was as it should be – made according to God's will – and everything was beautiful.

Friday arrived. Fortunately, the early summer weather held, and as before, Yankl, having picked up his violin, strolled with Velvel to the forest. As soon as the trees enfolded them, Velvel said: "Race you to our tree!" and started to run. Yankl gave chase, watching where he stepped to avoid falling with his precious instrument and damaging it. Velvel won the race with ease, reaching the glade with the big oak well before Yankl. He leaned against the tree, his arms by his side. Yankl came to a halt a few paces in front of him. "You are so handsome, Velvel."

"I love you, Yankl, just like Jonathan loved David." Yankl approached Velvel and caressed his cheek with his right hand. He leaned his body into Velvel's, coming to rest like a migrating bird after a long flight. He allowed himself the luxury of a long contented sigh.

Their love-making was even more passionate than it had been the first time, each now more familiar with what pleased the other. There was a relaxed feeling, a sharing of physicality, a giving and acceptance of gratification, and intense excitement.

Finally, peace spread over them, a sheltering canopy under the trees.

Yankl whispered: "I don't know what the future will bring us, Velvel, but I want you to know that at this moment, I cannot imagine being more happy." Velvel kissed the lobe of Yankl's ear and held him closer. "I pray it may last, and last, and last," he said.

They dressed. Velvel searched in his pocket for the little present he had brought for Yankl. He took out two cookies baked by his mother, carefully wrapped in a clean cloth. They gazed at the two perfectly round cookies touching each other on a bed of white linen, sharing the same thought. They looked into each other's eyes and recited the appropriate blessing: Blessed are you, O Lord our God, by whose word all things exist. They each ate one, savoring the different delicious sweetnesses as if they were an intrinsic part of their relationship.

"I have a present for you, too," said Yankl. "Close your eyes." Velvel did so. Yankl reached for his violin. He had composed a niggun especially for Velvel, but one that did not follow the traditional melody line.

He began with three loud chords. Then he started playing a very fast, quiet tune in a minor key with a vigorous, rhythmic beat. He repeated the melody, slightly louder and punctuated by the original three chords. The third time round, Yankl transposed the melody to a major key, running the bow over the strings with all his skill, stamping and jumping to the beat. He ended with the final three chords he had played at the beginning and shouting "Ya, ya, ya!" in time with the final notes.

Velvel jumped to his feet. "Wonderful! Wonderful!" he cried. "And that's for me?"

"Only for you!" said Yankl. "For nobody else, ever!"

They embraced, and remained holding each other. "How can I wait till next Friday?" said Velvel.

"Married couples wait two weeks after the woman's menstruation. We can wait one. Waiting will make it even better next Friday."

A pattern developed. Every Friday, Yankl would pick up his violin from home and walk with Velvel into the woods where they would renew their love for each other, physically, verbally and with music. Far from becoming a routine the habit strengthened their feelings for each other. Meanwhile, in the study hall, they continued to learn and absorb their heritage of Torah and Talmud, keeping their feelings strictly to themselves. They lived in three dimensions simultaneously: shabbes with their family; their days of study; and most intensely of all, the few hours they spent together in the forest accompanied by Yankl's violin melodies, Velvel's sweet voice and love. Never was a thought given to what they would do when the cold winds of winter arrived.

"Our love for each other was so intense, so complete," said Yankl "that I felt I had no right to expect it to last. I didn't dare to hope."

"It's a little like the history of our people," I said. "Hope and belief in the future have been the bywords of our people and 'hope' is

the word that most characterizes the Jewish soul. In fact, late in your life a most beautiful song was composed called 'hope' by a man named Naphtali Herz Imber. In Hebrew the word is 'Hatikvah', and the piece soon became the Jewish anthem. We must never stop hoping. There's always a glimmer of hope on the darkest night. We just have to find it, and never stop searching."

"For a while, I could see it and touch it," said Yankl as he continued his story.

Chapter 6

Yehudah Menke was a lonely boy. He was the third of eight siblings, but his closest older brother had been born five years before Yehudah's birth date, and following him came two sisters who enjoyed each other's company more than his. So Yehudah felt quite lonely. He competed for his parents' attention and when he succeeded in winning it, he suffered the jealousy of his closest brothers and sisters. He was not a happy child. Worse still, from the age of fourteen, his face had been plagued with irritating pimples that occasionally erupted into large red blotches on his skin.

Now, aged eighteen, Yehudah often felt depressed at home with nobody to talk to. On such occasions, he felt the need to leave the family house and just wander around, sometimes within the *shtetl*, sometimes in the surrounding forest.

One Friday afternoon in late summer, a few hours before the start of the Sabbath, Yehudah went walking in the woods. The sky was gray but there was no hint of rain in the air. Yehudah felt very sorry for himself. Perhaps his isolation would end when he was eventually married. But any girl would be repulsed by his awful skin condition, possibly to the point of not wanting to make love with him. He felt wretched. He hated his condition. He hated people. He hated the world. And he almost hated God. Instantly, he repented his sin begging the Divinity for forgiveness. After all, he still possessed all his limbs and all his faculties, and he was by no means stupid.

Suddenly, as Yehudah stepped between the trees, he heard the distant sound of a violin playing a beautiful melody with which he was familiar. It was a famous Yiddish lullaby, *Rozhinkes mit Mandlen* (raisons and almonds). Not wishing to interrupt the performance, but curious to see who was playing it, Yehudah approached the sound stealthily.

Yankl had picked up the melody by ear and taught himself to play it on his violin, as he had taught himself all the pieces he performed. Today, as he played, he sat on the ground, his legs stretched out in front of him and leaning his back against the tree trunk. Lying with his head in Yankl's lap was Velvel, his eyes closed and his left hand stretched out along Yankl's leg, holding his ankle.

Yehudah crept up and took in what, to him, was an unnatural situation. Velvel's red head of hair was resting on Yankl's thigh. And Yankl was virtually serenading him. Yehudah knew the two young men were chevrusas in the study hall but, he surmised, surely their intellectual activities could not extend this far.

The melody came to an end. Yankl placed his violin on the ground, then raised Velvel's head and kissed him gently on the lips, as if the action were an integral part of the musical composition.

Yehudah's left hand whipped up to his mouth to suppress his sharp intake of breath. Yankl and Velvel were acting like young lovers. Could this be? Male lovers? Yet his eyes were not betraying him. Yehudah realized with shock that he was indeed witnessing male lovers. He backed away, turned and avoiding any twigs that might snap beneath his feet, made his way back to the shtetl.

Yehudah was not at all disgusted by what he had seen. The scene was actually somewhat touching. In fact, the men of the shtetl were quite physical with each other. They often put their arms around each other's shoulders, held each other's hands as they whirled around in their dervish-like dances at family celebrations. In fact, on the festival of Purim celebrating the victory of Queen Esther and her uncle Mordechai over the wicked Haman, men helped each other home and even into bed after fulfilling the *mitzvah,* the divine commandment, of getting drunk – the only precept of its kind in the Jewish calendar.

But what Yehudah had seen went far beyond mere affection. A man kissing another man on the lips was unheard of and assuredly forbidden. And who knows what else they did with each other?

Yehudah was the first of his brothers to arrive home that afternoon. His two younger sisters were helping their mother prepare for the Sabbath.

"Mommeh," said Yehudah, "Guess what I found out."

"What might that be?" his mother asked.

"I can't tell you with Fraidel and Rachel here."

"Well, if you can't tell me with Fraidel and Rachel here, don't tell me at all," she said, casting Yehudah into deep frustration.

Hearing his deep sigh, his mother said: "So, go and tell your father instead of me, and he'll tell me later."

Yehudah's face brightened. He could still get the attention he sought so desperately. His Tatteh would listen to him. A half-hour later, Zelig Menke, Yehudah's father arrived home from his work. He had a dairy and kept his cows in a stable on the outskirts of the shtetl. He hardly had time to remove his jacket before Yehudah accosted him.

"Tatteh, guess what I found out."

"Yehudah, I'm tired. Do you want to tell me about it or don't you?"

"Yes, yes. But not here in the hallway, in my room."

Yehudah's father followed the young man into his sparsely furnished room. He had little patience to hear some unimportant fact that would bear no relevance at all to his life. They both sat on Yehudah's bed.

"Tell me quickly, Yehudah. I have to get ready for shabbes."

"Well," began Yehudah. "I was walking in the woods this afternoon, as I sometimes do. I was all alone and it was a nice day, but a bit cloudy." Yehudah's father sighed.

"Do I need to know about the weather?" he said impatiently. Yehudah ignored him.

"All of a sudden, I heard a violin being played and played very well. It was that melody we all know so well, the lullaby, *Rozhinkes mit Mandlen*."

"Yehudah," said his father, "Get on with it!"

"It was Yankl Bradawka, playing his violin. But," said Yehudah, pausing for effect, "he was not alone."

"So who was with him?"

"Velvel."

"Velvel. Velvel who?"

"Velvel Gambiner."

"So?"

"Velvel was with Yankl. Not just with Yankl. Yankl was sitting on the ground and Velvel was listening to him."

"So what's so special about that?"

"Velvel had his head in Yankl's lap."

Yehudah's father raised his head, his curiosity piqued. "Velvel could have just been resting and listening closely."

"Then they kissed."

A deep silence fell on the room. Yehudah's father stood up. He walked toward the door, not wanting to face this situation. He paced back into the room.

"What did you do?"

"I left. I came home." Yehudah was delighted with the effect his tale had had on his father. He had won his full attention. His father came and stood in front of him. Then he sat down again on the bed.

"Yehudah," he said. "Look at me. What is one of the worst sins in our religion?"

Yehudah thought for a moment. "Murder?"

"Yes, that's bad. But every bit as bad is murdering a personality through *loshon hora,* malicious gossip. Now I want you to promise me you'll say nothing of this to anybody. Not to anybody, do you hear me?" Zelig Menke raised his voice, angry that he would have to deal with this embarrassing situation and subconsciously blaming his son for it.

"Yes, Tatteh," replied Yehudah, his thoughts of getting attention from his siblings and fellow-students crashing to the ground.

"Promise me."

"I promise."

"And there's something else I need from you, something we must do together."

"What?" asked Yehudah, starting to wish that he had kept the incident to himself.

"I need to see for myself that what you've told me is the absolute truth. Not that Yankl was just playing his violin to Velvel, but that they did..." he hesitated, "...that they did what they did. Something... despicable. Now I know that the only time the two boys would have to be together, alone, is a Friday afternoon. So next Friday, I want you to take me to the spot where they met, and I want to see what happens there."

Yehudah blurted out: "But I told you exactly what I saw. You want to watch them with me, together?" Tears glistened in his eyes when the seriousness of his testimony dawned on him. Yehudah realized the implications. This was no longer a matter of attention-getting but of two lives, the lives of two virtual strangers, in the balance.

"Right, Yehudah. And if what you've told me is not true, or if I hear that you have repeated this story to anyone at all, and I *will* hear of it, I will send you away to a yeshiva in another city, far from here. Do you understand?"

"Yes, Tatteh."

His father stalked from the room, tired and angry that Yehudah should have put him in such a quandary. What could he do? What could he not do? He could hardly ignore the situation. How could two young men like Yankl and Velvel be in love with each other? Men did not marry men. How could that happen? It was not natural. How could they be stopped? Was he, a humble dairyman, responsible for the destiny of two young men whom he hardly knew? In fact, he had only a passing acquaintance with their parents. The only thing he could do was to bear witness to the truth himself.

The days of the week dragged by for both Zelig and Yehudah. At home, they consciously avoided each other, Zelig resenting the situation in which he found himself, and Yehudah realizing how serious the consequences of his attention-seeking could be. The boy wished fervently that he had said nothing to his father about what he had witnessed. More than that, he hoped against hope that Yankl and Velvel would, for some unknown reason, fail to make their way to their rendez-vous. Should he lead his father to some distant place in the forest, thought Yehudah, and claim that the young men had not put in their usual appearance? But that would only raise his father's suspicions and lay him open to the accusation of malicious gossip. He had no choice but to stand by his story.

During the hours of study, Yehudah would sometimes glance across the hall at Yankl and Velvel, discussing the Talmudic text, arguing, their hands gesticulating, Yankl's dark hair almost touching Velvel's red curls. From time to time, the two young men would break off their discussion to ponder a particularly thorny issue in the text, slowly twirling their side locks with their forefingers as they gave it some thought. Their relationship seemed so close, so harmonious. What was he about to destroy? Should he recant and tell his father he had fabricated the whole incident? But if he did that, his father's trust in him would vanish forever.

At the end of the week, early on Friday afternoon, Zelig and Yehudah walked into the forest. For a while, Yehudah wandered around, unsure of the precise location where Yankl and Velvel had met. The day was humid and it did not take long before father and son were sweating. Suddenly, above the rustling of the leaves, they heard the sound of a violin in the distance. They hid behind a tall bush as the sound approached. Then, through the trees, they saw Yankl walking and playing his violin. Behind him, Velvel followed, his right hand outstretched and resting on Yankl's shoulder, his left hand carrying Yankl's empty violin case. The two young men walked in step to the beat of the music, a version of the Marseillaise that had become very popular among Jewish musicians and music lovers. When they had passed, Zelig and Yehudah, the two spies, followed, far enough behind not to be heard, but close enough not to lose sight of their quarry.

Yankl and Velvel reached the glade that had become their love nest. Velvel gently took Yankl's violin and placed it in its case on the ground. The two men turned to each other and embraced, kissing with passion. As they started to remove each other's clothing, Zelig in his hiding place turned to his son and whispered: "Enough! We're leaving." Silently and slowly they moved, at first dodging from tree to tree to avoid detection, then hastening their pace to remove themselves from a scene that Zelig found disgusting, but that Yehudah found strangely intriguing.

"I've seen enough," said Zelig. "Now I have to decide what to do about it." Yehudah said nothing. He was overwhelmed by a feeling of remorse. He realized that he was instrumental in destroying something that, although quite out of the ordinary, nevertheless contained an element of beauty. The two young men had been so gentle with each other. But neither he nor the community into which he had been born could ever have imagined it as love.

Zelig, whose thinking was bounded by convention, his dairy and his home life, experienced only nausea at what he had seen. It was unnatural, a perversion of nature. He tried in vain to expel the vision he had just observed from his mind.

Shabbes was coming. He decided to sleep on the problem and do nothing for the present.

"How things have changed!" I said.

"In what way? I cannot believe that Jews now accept that men can love each other."

"Well, not ultra-Orthodox Jews. I think they accept that it can happen, but they still consider it a perversion. But today, in my world, there are many different types of Jews, some more liberal than others. And they are the majority. In their eyes, what happens between two men or two women in private is of no concern to them."

"How lucky you are," said Yankl. "Life must be so easy for you."

"In relative terms, it is, although some prejudice still exists. But you were fortunate enough to find someone who deserved your love and who returned it, a stroke of fortune as precious as a jewel. Even today, with all our modern contrivances, finding a soul mate is as hard as discovering that jewel. Many people, all types of people, live out their lives alone, too set in their ways to make compromises and too afraid of being hurt."

Chapter 7

When ordinary people come face to face with an insurmountable problem, they need advice. The oracle who dispensed this advice in the shtetl was the rabbi. Zelig Menke, the dairyman, realized that the problem of Yankl and Velvel was not one in which he could intervene personally. In fact, it was none of his business. Yet, as a person who considered himself a good Jew, neither could he ignore it. A good Jew took care of his fellow Jews. At the end of the shabbes morning service, he approached the rabbi.

"Rabbi Levy," he said, "I have a problem I need to discuss with you."

"Can it wait until tomorrow? It's shabbes. Unless it's urgent, of course."

"No. It's not so urgent."

"Come and see me tomorrow, just before ma'ariv."

While Yankl and Velvel slept innocently in their beds, their minds at peace and secure in each other's love, Zelig Menke spent the night tossing and turning, fearing the power he had to destroy two young lives but unable to accept their relationship. As day dawned, he rose, said his prayers, and set off mechanically to milk the cows and prepare the product of his work for sale to both the women of the town and to the local cheese-maker. At the end of his workday, he made his way to the shul to meet the rabbi.

In the rabbi's small study adjacent to the synagogue, Zelig reported what he and Yehudah had witnessed. Rabbi Levy could not believe what he was hearing. Zelig Menke fidgeted uncomfortably as the rabbi sat in shock for a few moments, incapable of responding. Yankl and Velvel were two of his star students in the yeshiva, committed, curious and intelligent. What would become of them if he took action as their rabbi? What would become of their families if their secret ever leaked out?

"Reb Zelig, this is a difficult problem, a problem we have to solve. But I, too, must think it over, and pray that the Holy One, Blessed be He, shows me the path to solve it. I ask you – no, I order you – not to breathe a word of this to anyone – not you nor your son. The solution must cause the least pain and suffering to everyone, especially the boys' families. Let me think. Let me pray for guidance. Let me take the necessary action. You have done well to come to me. Now it is no longer your problem. Forget that you and Yehudah ever saw anything. I will deal with it."

Zelig rose to leave. "Thank you, rabbi. I will do as you say, and I will make sure that Yehudah says nothing to anyone." Back on the street, Zelig Menke heaved a deep sigh of relief. He had passed the problem on. He and his son Yehudah were no longer responsible.

Alone, the rabbi leaned back in his seat, his elbows on the arms of the chair, hands touching, his fingers spread like an arrow pointing to heaven. He rested his chin on his outstretched thumbs, his index fingers against his lips. What a problem! He had no logical reason to doubt Zelig's word. Zelig had little contact with either of the boys' parents, and by nature, he was not in the least malicious. One thing was crystal clear to him: the boys must be separated, and as soon as possible. This sin could no longer be tolerated. But how to separate them? They lived in the same village and could not avoid seeing each other. Their parents would have to be told, but not at the same time. Each would blame the others' son for seducing their own. One of the boys would have to be sent away, to another town, to another yeshiva. So what to do with the other boy? Perhaps he would lead another young man astray.

Marriage. The thought struck him like a bolt of inspiration. Marriage. Yankl would have to get married and that would be an end to all his problems. It would be best to keep Yankl in Rypin, for with his musical gift, he was a far greater asset to the community than Velvel. Another reason why Velvel was the clear choice for banishment was that Yankl was an only son. To him alone fell the responsibility of producing children to perpetuate the family name. On the other hand, Velvel had two brothers who could fulfill that function should Velvel himself prove incapable of doing so.

How should he proceed? The first thing to do was to make arrangements for Velvel's departure to a yeshiva in another town. He would speak to the boy's parents, but they would have no choice in the matter.

Rabbi Levy immediately composed a letter to the head of the yeshiva in Vilna with whom he was acquainted. He explained in the vaguest of terms that Velvel had gone astray in his personal life and that he was obliged to leave his hometown. Nevertheless, he was a good student and deserved to pursue his studies for a few years before eventually marrying and taking up a trade. Rabbi Levy asked his colleague to explain the situation to the *mashgiach,* the assistant rabbi in charge of the students' ethical and moral welfare, who should keep an eye on the newcomer.

The next morning, Rabbi Levy gave the letter to one of his students to take to Dov Belman, the carter, who would deliver it to the nearest big town where it would be sent on its way via the inter-city coach to Vilna. The first step had been taken.

The rabbi now had to confront the parents, a most difficult task. How much should he tell them? Should he state the whole truth or prevaricate? He decided that any departure from reality would merely complicate the situation. He would first speak with Velvel's parents and try to cushion the blow of the loss of their son. At the end of the afternoon, he sent a boy to fetch Velvel's parents.

Sholom Gambiner was a stocky man, kept fit by the demands of his trade as the shtetl baker. He entered the small study followed by his wife, Golda, a strapping woman confident of her role as wife and mother, and the efficient running of her household. Strands of red hair poked out of the scarf she wore to cover her hair, the color a testimony to Velvel's family resemblance.

The couple sat down facing the rabbi across his desk, littered with documents and holy books. Apprehension was apparent on their faces.

"Has anything happened to Velvel?" asked his father.

"No," said the rabbi. "Nothing has happened to him and he is well. But..." He paused. "There is a problem." The atmosphere in the room chilled, as if a cold wave were about to crash down.

"I'll come straight to the point," he continued. "Velvel was seen in the forest." The rabbi took a deep breath. "He was seen with another boy. He was seen kissing that boy."

The boy's parents leaned back in their chairs. Velvel's father gripped the seat while his wife's hand shot up to cover her mouth.

"What? Where? Who? Who saw him? How? How could this happen? Boys don't kiss!" Mr. Gambiner spluttered.

"My son, my son," whispered his wife, "would never do such a thing. Velvel is a good boy." Her eyes brimmed with tears, her habitual self-confidence shattered.

"You don't know how sorry I am to have to break this dreadful news to you. Please believe me, Velvel is one of my best students. But I cannot doubt the source of this information. They were seen by reliable witnesses."

"What are we to do? Velvel must be sick. Can he be cured of this sickness?" Mr. Gambiner pondered the point, talking as if to himself. "Does our boy realize that his behavior is not normal? Does he know that you know?"

"No, Velvel knows nothing, and nor does he need to know. Nevertheless, there is a solution to this problem. I will not tell you the name of the young man he was seen with. It is not important for you to know that. But we must separate them. This cannot be allowed to continue. My solution is drastic and I hope you will accept it. We must send your boy away to another yeshiva in another city. For a while, you will be able to go and visit him perhaps once or twice a year. But he must have no contact with his friend. And we must do this as soon as possible."

Mrs. Gambiner looked stunned. "Sholom," she said, turning to her husband, "we are going to lose our son." Silent tears rolled down her cheeks. Mr. Gambiner put his head in his hands.

"Is there no other solution?" he muttered rhetorically.

"I can see no other way," said the rabbi. "Now, I don't think you should let the boy know the real reason why he is being sent away. Just tell him that the decision is mine and has been taken for the sake of his further education. He must leave as soon as possible. There is a wagon leaving tomorrow afternoon, and he should be on it. He will go to a yeshiva in Vilna where he will be well taken care of and be far from this evil distraction. Tomorrow morning before he leaves, I'll have a talk with him and explain the situation."

"So soon," moaned Velvel's mother.

"Aie, aie, aie. *Gevalt,*" said his father. "Such shame on our family."

"Now listen to me Reb Gambiner. There will be no shame. Nobody need know about this. The boy will be seen as going to an institution of higher learning in a bigger city. It will be considered a reward, a sort of scholarship. We'll tell people that a space has become available at another large yeshiva, which Velvel is privileged to fill. And another thing: when people ask you where Velvel has gone, tell them it's Warsaw. I don't want his accomplice in sin to find out where he's gone. He must not be able to contact him. That's all."

"And the other boy," said Mr. Gambiner. "Is he being sent away, too?"

"No," said Rabbi Levy. "I have found another solution for him, one that I shall insist he follow. But that is not a subject I want to discuss with you. But never fear, my decision as far as he is concerned will be just as effective as the one we have to make for Velvel."

Silence fell on the room, the decision hung over the three adults like a precariously balanced boulder. What have we done to deserve this? thought Mr. Gambiner. Where did we go wrong? thought Mrs. Gambiner. God in Heaven, thought the rabbi, why should such good people have to suffer so much?

"I wish you both a strong heart and lasting strength at this difficult time. You can tell Velvel what we have decided this evening. He is not to attend the study hall tomorrow morning but should come and see me. But make sure he is on the wagon leaving tomorrow afternoon." The rabbi stood.

Sholom Gambiner and his wife remained seated looking up at the rabbi, their faces streaked with tears.

"Is there no other way?" Velvel's father asked softly.

"No other way," replied the rabbi. "Take a few moments alone here before you leave. Compose yourselves. And I wish you joy and blessings from your other boys."

The rabbi left the couple in his office and walked into the shul. He sat in a pew, alone in the large, dark hall. He put his forearm on the back of the pew in front of him and rested his forehead on it. "Ribbonoh shel olom," he whispered, "Give them all the strength they need." When he returned to his office, Velvel's parents had left.

"They thought we were sick," explained Yankl. "We didn't feel sick. We just knew that we were different. If only they could have lived a day in our skin, they would have known."

"It took years, decades, more than a century, but eventually, even the psychiatrists, the mind doctors," I explained, "admitted that our sort of love was not a sickness, just a variant in the human

condition. Today, many countries protect our rights by law, although I don't suppose discrimination will ever be entirely eradicated. But great pain and a violent struggle had to occur before the change could happen. Most people now consider that we are absolutely normal."

"In my heart of hearts I have never felt anything else," said Yankl. I said nothing, but I looked again at his clothing, all black and white, the same as that still worn like a uniform by my ultra-orthodox co-religionists. Normalcy, I thought, is in the eye of the beholder.

Chapter 8

Velvel arrived home slightly later than usual. His father, as head of the family, would break the news to him so that it carried more authority.

As the evening meal progressed, Mr. and Mrs. Gambiner made great efforts to feign a normal attitude in front of their children. However, their thoughts were in turmoil. Mr. Gambiner contemplated his three sons, teasing each other and joking as they always did at the table.

"So," said Reuven, the oldest, "Velvel, how many new interpretations of the Talmud did you bring down today?"

"As many as the loaves of bread you baked," Velvel replied. "And you, Meir," said Velvel addressing the youngest in the family, "Have you learned *all* the laws of Pesach, the festival of Passover, yet?"

Is this the last happy meal we'll ever share together? thought Mr. Gambiner. The boys' mother thought: My son, my son, how can I lose him? What could he have done so wrong that the rabbi has to send him away? For both parents, the table scene seemed like a changeless image frozen in time. They struggled to compose the expression on their faces as their hearts wept, already mourning their middle son.

Following the evening meal, Mr. Gambiner said to Velvel: "Come, Velvel, we have to discuss something together. Let's sit outside on the bench in the back."

Velvel had little time to wonder whether anything was wrong. The two men sat on the bench.

"I saw Rabbi Levy today," began Mr. Gambiner. "He said there is a wonderful opportunity for you and your studies. There is a place for you at the yeshiva in Vilna where you will have the finest rabbis and students to study with."

Velvel's heart sank. 'Yankl, Yankl, Yankl,' clanged through his brain like an alarm bell. He was going to lose his beloved Yankl...

"But, Tatteh, I'm happy here," he almost pleaded.

"Sometimes, Velvel, we have to make difficult decisions for the sake of our future. Rabbi Levy thinks you are ready for Vilna. You will be exposed to the most brilliant minds of our times. Your future will be enriched by such teachers."

Velvel panicked. What excuse could he find not to go? "But I'll be away from you and Mommeh?"

"Velvel, you're a man now. We'll come and visit you at least twice a year. You'll see, after a few weeks, you'll feel completely at home there. Mommeh is packing a few clothes for you, and you'll leave tomorrow afternoon. In the morning, you will go and bid goodbye to Rabbi Levy, and I'll give you a few books that you can take with you."

"So soon?" He echoed his mother's words. He would not even have time to say goodbye to Yankl. He would just disappear. It would be as if their love had never happened; it would be wiped out. Why the haste? Could someone have seen them together and told the rabbi?

"Let me think about this alone for a few minutes," he said to his father.

"Not too long. You must go to bed early tonight. Tomorrow will be a long day."

"Very good Tatteh." His father slowly turned and went back into the house, heavy-hearted.

Velvel remained sitting on the bench. His questioning turned to concern. What would Yankl think when he disappeared? Would he feel betrayed? His concern turned to fear. How would he manage in the future without Yankl? How would he live? Then anger. How could they do this to him? And what would become of Yankl?

He had to see him and tell him what was happening. He stood up, and then sat down again. He imagined the scene as he reached Yankl's house. He saw himself standing on the Bradawkas' doorstep asking to see Yankl. Yankl coming to the door. Velvel's own tears rolling down his cheeks as he stood facing the man he loved, speechless, incapable of explaining the hopeless situation to him. Yankl would be alarmed and not know how to react. If he left the house with Velvel, he would have to make excuses to his parents, and invent a plausible explanation. The prospect was just too daunting to contemplate.

Once more, Velvel stood up. He could not face it. He stepped out of the backyard. It was still light although the sun had set. Velvel walked through the back lane and the emptying streets, into the woods, his heart pumping with emotion. He felt his entire world had collapsed. His helplessness turned to despair and in the lowering dusk the trees seemed to embrace him, comforting him. He lay down under a big tree listening to the breeze rustling the leaves. The full implication of a future without Yankl suddenly struck him and he let out a long, mournful wail as sobs wracked his body. He sat up and wrapped his arms around his body. "No, no, no, no," he cried. "Why? What have I done to deserve this?" He could see no solution. Like feathers flying from a burst pillow, his life was in tatters.

Chapter 9

The next morning, Yankl entered the study hall, eager to see his chevrusa once again. Instead, he found a note lying on the desk that they shared. It read:

> *Your chevrusa, Velvel, has a slight fever. Please join two other students on a temporary basis until he recovers.*
>
> *Rabbi Levy*

In his note, Rabbi Levy had felt obliged to lie. Velvel had no fever. But, he rationalized, he was indeed sick. His behavior with Yankl proved that he was not well and in an unnatural state of being that had to be changed. Yet, should he expel Velvel only to impose him and his perverted desires on other innocent students elsewhere? Nevertheless, reflected the rabbi, Velvel had not acted alone in this matter. Yankl was as much to blame as he was. It was not as if either boy had attempted to seduce any other unsuspecting victim. Deep in the rabbi's consciousness was the realization that this affair was not one of deviant lust only, a thought he instantly dismissed as being impossible. He would be gentle with Velvel, but firm.

Velvel knocked on the rabbi's door and walked in. His face was paler than usual and his fatigue was evident.

"Sit down, Velvel. I believe your parents have explained this wonderful opportunity that has arisen for you. There is a free place for you at the yeshiva in Vilna. You will be able to study with the finest minds in this part of the world. I hope that you appreciate what this means for you."

Velvel looked at the rabbi. He coughed nervously.

"Rabbi, I am happy here. I am doing so well with my chevrusa, Yankl, learning so much. Could I not stay for just a few more months?"

"Velvel, you know that if you do not take this place, someone else will, and it could be months before another opening occurs."

A thought struck Velvel. "Do I have any choice in this matter?"

The rabbi paused before answering. "No," he said bluntly.

"Rabbi," said Velvel, "I must ask you another question. Is there any other reason why you are sending me to Vilna?"

The moment of truth had arrived for Rabbi Levy. How would the young man react? He paused before answering.

"Velvel, yes, there is another reason. You must understand that you are afflicted with a serious condition that we must overcome. You were seen with Yankl, your chevrusa, in the forest, and you were not studying Talmud or Torah." Velvel blanched, then blushed deeply.

"Seen?" he whispered.

"Velvel, your secret has been discovered. It is still known to just a few people and it must remain so. But it cannot be allowed to continue. You have to leave, and as soon as possible. That is why you must take the cart out of Rypin this afternoon. I hope and pray that in Vilna you will find the right way, God's way, to live your life."

Velvel sat back in his chair. There was no hope whatsoever. "Can I at least say goodbye to Yankl?"

"No," said the rabbi sternly. "I shall say goodbye to him for you. Any future contact between you is forbidden. You must repent, not be placed in the way of temptation. Change your ways and you will be happy. Pursue the path of sin and you will be cursed."

"But what will happen to Yankl?"

"That is not your concern. I have decided on a course of action that will correct the flaw in his character, too. Now leave. I hope you have the will to change and lead a life of blessing."

Velvel rose unsteadily. He feared not only his own fate but Yankl's, too. What cruel destiny had the rabbi planned for him? Velvel left the rabbi's office and walked home in a daze. His future was out of his hands, the decision taken by others. He entered the family home and sat at the kitchen table. The house was empty. He rested his head on his hands, too stunned even to cry. "Not even allowed to say goodbye," he said aloud.

He looked up and around him. Would he ever see these walls again? He tried to engrave the image of this family room on his brain so that he would remember it in his lonely moments in Vilna. The large wooden kitchen table where the family took their meals. The lofty cabinet containing the plates and cutlery, stored on separate shelves and in different drawers for meat and dairy dishes. The stove with the range for cooking. And two armchairs, one larger than the other for his parents' moments of relaxation, mainly on the Sabbath.

The door at the back of the house clicked open, stirring him from his reverie. His mother entered with food for the family's evening meal. She placed her purchases in the larder behind the kitchen and entered the room. Velvel, still seated at the table with his head resting on his hands, thought of last evening's meal, probably the last he would share with any family that he could call his own. His mother sat down opposite him.

"Velvel," she said. He did not move his head. "Velvel, we love you."

He looked at her as if suddenly surprised entered her presence. "Oh. Yes," he said, "I know." Mrs. Gambiner took in her son's depressed mood. Surely, if the accusation against him had been groundless, he would have seized this opportunity to go to Vilna with joy. She realized that the rabbi had told her son the real reason for his move.

"Did you not realize what your behavior would do to us all?" she said. "To us, your parents, your brothers, and to yourself? Your father and I were forced to agree with this decision. What else could we do? You cannot believe that we really want to send you away. We have no choice. It's for your own good. You know that what you've been doing is wrong."

"Wrong? Why wrong?" Velvel leaned back in his chair and closed his eyes. He spoke as if his mother were not there. "What 'wrong' were we doing to anyone? Just because it is written that we are wrong, are we wrong? Who made us like this? Who cursed us like this? How can love be wrong? I don't understand. I don't understand anything." Silent tears rolled down his cheeks.

"Velvel, Velvel," his mother rocked backward and forward in her chair. "I don't understand either. Two men cannot love each other. How could that be?" Silence descended upon them like a falling barrier as they each retreated into their own opposing worlds. A few moments passed. "Never forget that we love you," said his mother as her own tears brimmed over.

She dried her eyes. "Come. I've prepared a bag with your clothes and a few of your father's books, and I have some food and a little money for your journey. Your father could not leave the bakery but he will write you. He loves you, too, you know."

"Tell me, Mommeh, does loving someone mean having to make them unhappy?"

Mrs. Gambiner shared her son's pain, feeling it as intensely as if it were her own. "Velvel, I cannot answer that question. In our world, this is the way things are. This is the way things have to be. Nobody wants to send you away, but we cannot accept this situation. You must go and learn to see things differently. And we must all try and forgive each other for what is happening. All I ask of you now is that, for the sake of the family, you try to show some dignity."

Velvel wiped his face with his kerchief. He took the bag that his mother had fetched from a corner of the room, the money and the package of food containing some of his favorite homemade cookies, and walked slowly with his mother to the inn from where the cart to the next city departed. They each savored the painful moment in silence, knowing that it might be their last together for a long time. The wagon was waiting. Velvel kissed his mother and hugged her.

"Yes," he said, "we must all try to forgive each other."

"God bless you, Velvel," his mother whispered. Velvel put his packages in the cart, climbed in and sat on the bench attached to the side of the vehicle, staring straight ahead. He was the only passenger. The wagon pulled away, the crunching of the wheels on the road feeling like darts piercing his heart. Velvel did not look back. His mother waved her kerchief as the tears finally flowed freely down her distraught face.

Chapter 10

Rabbi Levy's painful duty was not finished. He now had to face Yankl's parents and confront them with the distressing reality. Yankl would accept Velvel's absence for another day before becoming anxious and concerned. In the meantime, the rabbi would have to put things to rights with his parents. Early that evening, he summoned Yankl's parents to his study.

Rabbi Levy had the experience of déjà vu as the Bradawkas walked through the door. Mendl Bradawka was a sturdy, strong man, which he needed to be as the shtetl butcher. His wife, Leah, was as tall as he, a woman with a refined face, and a less heavy figure than most of the women in the community. They sat down, equally as nervous as the Gambiner parents had been. Being called to the rabbi's office was rarely to receive good news.

"Reb Bradawka," said the rabbi, using the respectful form of 'Mr.'. "You and Mrs. Bradawka must realize that this is not a happy occasion," he began. "I am very concerned about your son, Yankl."

"What has he done?" said Mendl Bradawka, concerned.

"Well, I ask myself what will become of him."

"Please explain, rabbi," said Leah Bradawka.

Wishing to be as gentle as he could, the rabbi said: "Your son is a very talented young man, in many ways. He is a bright, intelligent student and an accomplished musician. But there is one aspect of his character that we must try to correct." He paused, uneasy with the need to cause pain.

"Go on, rabbi," said Mr. Bradawka.

"Your son was seen in the forest with another of my students playing his violin. Not only playing his violin. He was seen kissing his companion."

The shock was palpable.

"Nu," said Mr. Bradawka, searching desperately for a logical explanation, "Sometimes we get carried away by affection and…"

"On the lips, Reb Bradawka," interrupted the rabbi.

"God in heaven," muttered Yankl's father. Mrs. Bradawka was almost too upset to cry although her eyes suddenly became moist.

"What are we to do?" she said. "Which boy?"

"I will not tell you which boy, although later you may realize who it is. What I will tell you is that his parents are just as disturbed by all this as you are, and you must not blame them or their son for this. Both boys are adults and responsible for their actions, and both must suffer the consequences."

"What consequences?" said Yankl's father.

"I have given this situation very careful thought. There is a solution for Yankl that would leave everyone happy: marriage. Yankl must marry. He is of the right age, and once he finds true happiness with a wife, his problem will disappear. I guarantee that we can find a nice girl for him, a girl from a good family who will make a fine mother for his children. It should not be difficult to find someone suitable, Yankl is an attractive, intelligent young man and any girl would be proud to have him as the head of her family. However, what I want you to do is convince Yankl that marriage is the right thing for him. Can I rely on you to do that?"

"Of course, rabbi," said Mr. Bradawka. "You can rely on me to persuade Yankl to do what's best. What's best for him, too."

"As for me," the rabbi continued, "you can rely on me to keep this distressing matter confidential. This sin must not become known to the community. The results could be disastrous. Two young men, from good families pursuing immorality... what an example to set for the innocent young!"

Mrs. Bradawka came out of her shock. "He's always been such a good boy. Immoral? I cannot imagine my Yankl being immoral."

The rabbi bristled. "It is an abomination. The Torah states that it is an abomination! We all face temptations, but with God's help we overcome them. God has given us free will, the choice to do what is right or what is wrong. We all have choices to make. In this, Yankl has made the wrong choice. He must be shown the right way, and marriage is the way to do it."

Mendl Bradawka, aware of the rabbi's growing anger, sought to calm him. "Rabbi, I have said that I will convince him that your solution is the right one. Don't worry, this upsetting situation will all work out for the best. I had not thought of speaking to Yankl about marriage for a year or two, but the moment has obviously come. I will speak with him tonight."

"Meanwhile, Mrs. Bradawka, " the rabbi continued, "I want you to talk to Mrs. Haizerick, the *shadchan*, the matchmaker, and ask her to find a suitable young woman to be Yankl's wife. You can then arrange a meeting between the girl she finds and Yankl, together with the girl's parents. Of course, not a word is to be said to them or to anyone else about this unfortunate incident. That would end the arrangement before it began. We will remain in touch with each other, and I shall expect Yankl to make every effort to make this solution work. With God's help, we can turn this curse into a blessing." The Bradawkas left the rabbi's study and the rabbi sighed with relief. The worst was over. He had succeeded in convincing both sets of parents that separation on the one hand, and marriage on the other would remove the evil eye from his congregation. He muttered a silent prayer to God, thanking Him for His guidance in this terrible dilemma.

Yankl arrived home at the usual time after his day of study. The day had not been routine. Studying with two other students instead of one had been confusing as it meant having to respond to two arguments instead of one. His head was buzzing with all the talk and cross-talk. As he stepped over the threshold, he was immediately struck by the tension in the air. His father had not yet ended his workday, but his mother bustled around the kitchen, clattering pots and pans as if she wished to avoid talking to him.

"Mommeh, is anything the matter?"

"No, Yankl. What should be the matter?" She averted her eyes.

"No, nothing. Velvel was sick today and didn't come to the yeshiva."

"Oh?" she said, her suspicions aroused.

"I was stuck with two other students, which wasn't the same as usual. I hope Velvel's all right."

Leah Bradawka said nothing. Yankl went to his room, a strange look on his face. A few minutes later, his father came home.

"Tatteh," his wife used the name everyone called him in the family, "Velvel, Yankl's chevrusa was not in the study hall today. Do you think that means something?"

Mendl Bradawka scratched his beard. "Yes, perhaps. The rabbi didn't say what the consequences would be for the other boy. Perhaps he told him to stay home to keep them apart. After all that's happened, the rabbi would not want there to be any contact between them. We'll see in the next day or so whether that's the case."

Yankl could hear them talking in low tones downstairs. A seed of anxiety took root in his mind. Velvel's absence. His mother's mood. Quiet voices. He uttered a silent prayer that nothing had gone wrong.

The evening meal was a subdued affair. The table talk was usually animated, with Mendl Bradawka asking his son and daughters how their day had passed, what they had learned, and whom they had met. However, not every evening was as lively as others, and Yankl tried to convince himself that his parents had had a busy day and were tired. The illusion was shattered as the meal came to an end. Following the short grace after meals, Mendl Bradawka said to his son: "Yankl, your mother and I have something to talk to you about. Girls, go to your room and read a book. Your mother will be up soon to put you to bed."

Yankl's two sisters scampered up to the room they shared, happy to escape their parents' supervision. After clearing the table, the three adults sat down in their places, Yankl on one side, his parents on the other. Yankl imagined a sudden echo of the word 'Inquisition'.

"Yankl," said Mr. Bradawka, "today we saw Rabbi Levy, and naturally, we talked about the progress you're making and about your future. Both we and the rabbi think that you have spent enough time studying. We have to think of your long-term future. You have a talent that can obviously be exploited as a profession – your music. You can continue to perform at *simchas,* family celebrations, and you could even give lessons to children, in both violin and Jewish studies. But you must also think of starting a family."

Yankl's face blanched. His father continued. "Now, we are going to find a nice young girl for you, a suitable girl for you to marry. Yankl, it's time we became grandparents." He smiled at his son.

Yankl's thoughts churned. First, no Velvel. What had they done with Velvel? Perhaps he really was sick. And now, marriage. How could he think of marriage? What were his parents trying to get him into? Play along, he told himself.

"But Mommeh, Tatteh, I want to continue at the yeshiva. I'm doing so well with my chevrusa."

Suspicion crossed the mind of both his parents: it must be Velvel who was Yankl's partner in sin. Mendl Bradawka pictured the shame that would befall his family should his son's secret become known. First, his business would shrink;

he and his wife would be shunned by the community; his daughters would be ostracized and unable to find husbands. All the pressure of the last few hours hit him like an avalanche. His world seemed in danger of being shattered. How could his son commit such a sin? How could he embark on such an outrageous course of action? Had he no respect for his family?

Mendl Bradawka stood. The anxiety caused to him and his wife exploded in an outburst of anger. He brought his fists down on the table with a resounding crash, making his wife and son jump with fright. He bellowed: "Yankl, you will get married, and as soon as possible! Do you hear me?"

His wife started to cry, fearful of what the future would bring and finally allowing herself the relief of tears. Yankl was speechless. He felt his parents' pain as he became aware of the nausea in the pit of his stomach. Yet all he could think of was Velvel.

"Where is Velvel?" he asked, his voice shaking.

His father glared at him. "I don't care a jot for Velvel. I care about you. I care about this family. I care about the future." He raised his voice. "Yankl, I'm telling you, you *will* get married. How did all this business start anyway? Did Velvel lead you astray?"

Yankl could see no point in lying. "It just happened," said Yankl. "We didn't plan it. We couldn't help it."

"Well," said his father, "there's an end to this disgusting sin. I don't think you'll be seeing much of Velvel again from now on. And once you're married, we'll have solved the problem once and for all."

Yankl was broken. Nobody understood, and nobody could understand. He saw no choice. The future would be miserable, married to a woman with whom he could not make love. Strangely, when he thought of relations with a woman, the word his father had just used, 'disgusting', flashed through his mind. For him, the act would be totally unnatural, no matter how much affection he might feel for his spouse. But, he thought, defiantly, if unhappiness is what they all want, unhappiness is what they will get. He realized that trying to explain would be a fruitless task. After all, they considered what he and Velvel had done to be a mortal sin.

"Very well, Tatteh. I'll do as you wish," he said in a low voice.

"Yankl," said his mother gently, "you can be sure that the girl we choose will be attractive and make you a good wife. We're not asking you to marry just anyone. She'll come from a good family and you'll have beautiful children."

"Yes, Mommeh." But where was Velvel? "May I go to my room now?"

"Yes, Yankl," said his father sitting down. "And we'll all dance at your wedding. You'll see, everything will turn out well, with God's help."

God's curse, Yankl said to himself, feeling guilty for the blasphemous thought as soon as it entered his head.

As he walked to the study hall the next morning, Yankl hoped against hope that Velvel's smiling face would be there to greet him. Instead, he found a note from Rabbi Levy: Velvel has been sent to a yeshiva in another city to advance his studies. Shloime Goldfarb will be your new chevrusa.

Shloime Goldfarb. All Yankl wanted to do was grieve. There had been so many years of loneliness and isolation. Eliyohu had not understood. Avrum had betrayed both him and his own wife. Finally, with Velvel, relief had come, communication had come, love had come. Now Yankl had to prepare himself for a loveless marriage that would make both him and his future wife completely miserable. The mental pain numbed him and he functioned as he had always done, but like a clockwork clown, as if another person had taken over his thoughts.

"Rabbi Shimon said in the name of Rabbi Tarphon..." he droned the texts automatically, focussing his attention on proposing and responding to arguments, and willing himself to shut out his own life. Somehow he managed to get through the day, counting the hours and minutes when he would finally be alone in his own room, lying on his bed and able to let the silent tears flow.

Friday came around and, as usual, he took his violin into the woods. Just one week before, Velvel had been by his side. Yankl reached the spot where they had spent so many wonderful times together, talking, dancing to his violin music and making love. He could almost hear Velvel's voice, laughing, singing, teasing him. Now Yankl did not even know to which city he had been banished. He looked around the glade where they had snatched such precious moments from their daily routine. Someone – Yankl had no idea who – had concealed himself among these trees and carried back the tale of their liaison. In a strange way, Yankl could almost sympathize with the talebearer. What he and Velvel had found in each other was something unheard of in their community. Something extraordinary. As such, it challenged the conventional standards of the shtetl. How could anyone understand?

Loneliness flooded over him like a sudden summer squall. Yankl sat down, his back against a tree, savoring the memories and wishing he could turn the clock back. He inhaled the fresh smell of the trees, taking deep breaths. How could he mourn a lost lover? What ritual was there to follow? The answer slowly emerged from his confused thoughts. *Keriyah* was the symbolic gesture of tearing a garment to express bereavement, representing the sackcloth of Biblical times. He would do it. He removed his shirt. The garment underneath, worn between his shirt and his undershirt was the *tsitsis,* a rectangular piece of cloth with a circular hole in the center for the head to pass through, and with four specially woven tassels on each corner. Orthodox Jewish men wore it with the tassels protruding beneath their shirt as a constant reminder of God and of their own Jewish place in His world. Yankl lifted it over his head and laid it down on top of his shirt.

Realizing that no visible sign of mourning would be acceptable, Yankl tore a slit in the neckline of his tsitsis. He kissed the holy garment, replaced it over his head and pulled his shirt back on again. He lifted his violin. "This is for you Velvel," he said "wherever you are." He caressed the strings to the melody of another song from their shared heritage, *Yedid Nefesh,* Kindred spirit. The haunting melody, customarily chanted at the end of the Sabbath, was one that Velvel had sung to Yankl's accompaniment. As the last notes faded away, Yankl said: "Let us both be strong for each other." He looked around the glade to imprint it on his memory, and walking backward toward the trees, left it for the last time.

Yankl paused, reminiscing. "I had plunged from heaven to hell. As quickly as we had found each other, so we lost each other. But looking back, I realize how very lucky we had been – to know that we both existed, that we both wanted the same thing, and that we had enjoyed those few precious months in each other's company. It was a time of total fulfillment that I treasured for the rest of my days. And for which I thanked God."

Chapter 11

Mrs. Haizerick was a stereotype – a shadchan and a *yenta*, a gossip. She had to know everyone's business before they knew it themselves, and she was convinced that she knew how to solve all their problems. Her own principal problem was that nobody listened to her. She lived in a one-room hut, cold in winter so that she had to wear several layers of clothing, and hot in summer, which drove her outside and into any store or home that would accommodate her and offer her a cool drink. Her husband had died young following an extended bout with tuberculosis, leaving her with three young boys whom she had struggled to feed, with some support from the community. By some miracle, her husband Hymie's malady had not infected the other members of his family.

In his day, Hymie's suffering had been attributable not only to his poor physical condition but also to his wife's clacking tongue. Perhaps as an antidote to both, he had established a reputation that equaled that of his wife, but for a completely different reason. Hymie Haizerick was a short man whose slender body was always preceded by a belly totally out of proportion to the rest of his build. And matching this particular feature was a voice as deep and loud as a foghorn. Unfortunately, he was also slightly deaf in one ear – perhaps out of necessity – and tone deaf in both.

None of this would have mattered had Hymie Haizerick not used his voice to full and ill effect. Every Friday evening, there was a point toward the end of the shul service inaugurating the Sabbath when the cantor paused to take breath before chanting the next melody. The congregation then joined in. It was Hymie's custom to cut in, just before the cantor began, and in his booming voice, start singing the melody in a key quite beyond the cantor's range. After the first few notes, the notion of correct pitch in his singing became one of pure coincidence. Inevitably the melody had then to be 'rescued' by the cantor who, after several months of bearing this humiliation, succeeded in bringing it to an end in the following manner.

One Friday evening, as the congregational song closed, the cantor turned around to face the worshippers and addressed Hymie Haizerick directly.

"Mr. Haizerick, since you take such pleasure in leading the service when it's almost over, perhaps you'd like to lead it from the start!" Hymie Haizerick flushed, but that was the last time that he ventured into the realm of cantorial performance.

When the Haizerick boys were grown and married, they left the family home and moved to Warsaw. Their widowed mother then took up her business of matchmaking, boasting endlessly about her 'contacts'.

In the absence of her late departed husband and her boys, Mrs. Haizerick was naturally a very lonely woman. She hated the smallness and the silence of the little home into which she had been obliged to move and, unable to chat to anyone within it, she talked to herself. Yet she was far from stupid. She reasoned that she had enjoyed good times with her husband and children and now she would help others to do so. Occasionally, parents would themselves arrange a wedding for their eligible children, but if that option were not available, they would turn to the services of the shadchan. When matching single young people for what she hoped would be a shared life of harmony, Mrs. Haizerick had to consider the families they came from. Indeed, she almost had to match the parents of the bride and groom as well as the young couple, a feat she usually achieved, but not always. On the other hand, her rare failures in that respect gave her good cause for complaint, the pursuit of laying blame giving her only slightly less pleasure than arranging a blessed marriage.

As Leah Bradawka approached Mrs. Haizerick's house, she felt torn by her emotions. Although she wanted nothing more than her son's happiness, she had the profound feeling that marriage would not be the solution to his problems. Months, even years before, her maternal instinct had warned her that not all was as it should be with Yankl, although she was unable to put her finger on precisely what was wrong. All she knew was that her son was trying to conceal his unhappiness. Nevertheless, his sin with Velvel was unforgivable, incomprehensible and shameful. She had to find the right girl to distract him and help him overcome his misguided inclinations, a very special girl. These were her thoughts as she walked up to Mrs. Haizerick's shack.

"Come in, dear," said Mrs. Haizerick, welcoming Mrs. Bradawka. "Sit down. What can I do for you?" she asked, knowing the answer full well. Leah Bradawka sat on the one rickety chair in the room while the shadchan sat on her bed.

"It's Yankl, my son."

"Ah, yes, Yankl. A handsome boy, an intelligent boy. And such a musician! The way his fingers fly over those strings, the dream of every daughter's mother. And every mother's daughter." She laughed gaily at her much-practiced attempt at witticism. "I've watched him grow up from when he was a little boy..." Her words streamed on like an eternal fountain as Yankl's mother asked herself whether her son's and family's happiness was worth sitting through the flood spouting from this blabbermouth. After a few minutes she interrupted.

"Mrs. Haizerick, I've come to find a wife for Yankl. He's ready to get married. Do you know of anyone suitable?"

"Suitable? Of course, I can find someone suitable for a young man like that, and so eligible. Let me see." Mrs. Haizerick fell into a sort of trance, her hand over her eyes. She talked to herself softly. "There's the Pincus girl. Too short. The Lifshitz girl. Hmmm. The family there, I'm not too sure. Ah!"

she cried. "The Schneider girl. Her mother hasn't been to see me yet, but I've been watching that girl. Yes, yes, yes. I think she'd be ideal. A beautiful girl. Intelligent, too. A good family. Yes, let me speak to Mrs. Schneider."

Leah Bradawka was familiar with the Schneider family. They lived on a small farm at the edge of the shtetl and the father supplied the community with eggs, dairy foods and vegetables in season. Leah Bradawka did not know the girl, but she knew the family had a good name. She only hoped that the girl would please Yankl.

"Very well, Mrs. Haizerick. Let's arrange for them to come and see us. The girl and her parents."

As she left the matchmaker's small house, Leah Bradawka was overcome with a feeling of apprehension. Life was full of uncertainty, and this was no ordinary match. Yankl had been caught in the act of kissing a man and had confessed to committing the sin. Worse still, he had expressed no remorse for his action, merely agreeing under pressure to get married. She wondered whether marriage would succeed in turning Yankl away from his desire for another man. And did he desire men instinctively, or was it only Velvel in particular that had attracted him? Perhaps her son should remain single like her American uncle, Aaron, despite all the opprobrium that such a state would bring down on his and his family's head. After all, disapproval was not condemnation and, provided his sick desire for a relationship with a man remained secret, his single status would, at least, not involve a scandal or worse. She realized that she had no choice. As a mere woman, she could hardly oppose the will of her husband or the rabbi. This way had to be tried, despite the possible failure of the marriage. Even the slimmest chance of success had to be grasped.

She tried to see the situation in a more optimistic light. If her husband and the rabbi were right, Yankl would get married, fall in love with his wife, and produce beautiful and talented grandchildren for her and her husband.

Two weeks passed. Yankl maintained his impassive front, seeming to accept the end of his relationship with Velvel as inevitable. But at night, alone on his bed, he gave vent to his grief, mixed with anger at not having even been given the opportunity to bid Velvel farewell. His new chevrusa, Shloime Goldfarb, was as alive and meaningful to him as the chair he sat upon. Velvel's beautiful eyes smiled at him in his dreams. It was as if Yankl lived in two worlds, one, lifeless, when he was awake, and the other, full of joy and music in his nocturnal fantasies. Then, everything changed.

On arriving home from the study hall one evening, Yankl's father greeted him with a smile.

"Yankl, we have good news for you. Your mother has been to see Mrs. Haizerick, the shadchan, and she has found a beautiful girl for you to meet."

"Oh," said Yankl flatly.

"Her name is Naomi Schneider and she and her parents are coming to meet us tomorrow evening. Your mother and I are looking forward to meeting them. Rabbi Levy tells me the girl comes from a good family, and she's bright and ready to get married."

"Yes, Tatteh." Yankl could think of nothing else to say. Behind his eyes, little demons chased one another in frantic circles crying to each other: How could *he* get married? How could *he* get married? Yankl felt a devilish power manipulating him like a marionette, forcing him to do something that was against his very nature. He was totally powerless.

As the next day dawned, Yankl regained consciousness with a feeling of nausea and foreboding as he realized what the day would bring. His obsession with memories of the recent past was replaced by preoccupation with the future. He imagined himself on his wedding night, lying next to his bride, she fearful of a potentially brutal assault on her virginity, and he terrified of his inability to perform what was expected of him. The image sickened him. Somehow, he would battle through.

As he arrived home after his day in the study hall, Yankl could hear the sounds of conversation drifting through the front window of the house. The Schneiders had arrived. On entering the living room, he took in the view of his potential parents-in-law. Otto Schneider was somewhat shorter than Yankl's father. He had a kindly face with eyes that twinkled above a large, black beard. His wife, Hannah, had kept her good looks. She was slightly built with a wisp of hair, still brown, poking out from the scarf on her head. Yankl was introduced. He shook hands with Mr. Schneider and inclined his head toward Mrs. Schneider. Naomi, their daughter, was seated in the corner, playing with Esther and Rivka, Yankl's younger sisters.

After her parents were introduced to Yankl, Naomi rose shyly from her chair. Without doubt, she was a beauty, tall, slim, her face with a bone-china complexion enhanced by a halo of brown curls. She smiled at Yankl. "Good evening, Yankl," she said.

Yankl forced himself to smile back as he returned her greeting. Wishing to avoid any awkward silence, Mr. Schneider said: "We hear you're not only an excellent violinist, Yankl, but a very fine yeshiva student, too."

"I do my best," Yankl responded. Then, a thought struck him: if he could make himself appear unattractive to his intended life partner, perhaps she would refuse him. At least, that would give him some breathing space. He added: "But both my music and my Talmud studies could be much improved."

"You are too modest," said Mrs. Schneider. "We have been so looking forward to meeting you, and we have heard only good things of you. I know your parents are very proud of you. Our daughter, Naomi is something of a musician, too. My great aunt left us her piano when she passed on, and Naomi is quite an accomplished player. So we'll look forward to listening to the two of you giving us a concert." She laughed happily, clearly excited at the prospect of having this handsome young man as her son-in-law. She was sure he would make her beloved daughter happy.

"The Schneiders are staying with us for supper," Leah Bradawka informed Yankl. "So Mrs. Schneider will help me prepare, and the men will go and chat in the backyard. You and Naomi can get to know each other in here. We'll be just in the next room if you need anything."

"A glass of water, please, Mommeh," said Yankl nervously. Fantasies bombarded his head. Naomi, was beautiful. He liked her, almost loved her, at first sight. Then he imagined, horrified, being alone in bed with her. He just wanted to be her friend, nothing more. Then he told himself: keep up the family name. You're a Bradawka. You cannot ruin the family honor. Play the game.

His mother brought a glass of water for both Yankl and Naomi as her daughters ran up to their room to play. The two sets of parents then left the young couple alone.

"How long have you been playing the violin?" Naomi's voice was like velvet, soft and smooth.

"Since I was six. And you, have you been playing the piano for long?"

"Since I was six." They both laughed. There seemed to be an instant complicity between them. Yankl cursed his fate. This girl would have made the ideal wife for him.

"Isn't this a strange ritual we go through?" said Yankl. "We meet once and then we're supposed to get married and live together in instant bliss."

"Well, it may not be instant. But if we both try hard, I'm sure it will work. Just look at my parents, and probably your parents, too. They didn't know each other before they got married. And they all seem very happy together."

"But we know so little of each other beyond what we look like. Yes, you know I play the violin and that I go to the yeshiva, but how do you know what I'm really like? Will I be easy to live with?" He tried to raise doubts in Naomi's mind.

"How do you know I'm not temperamental, suffering from moods, or untidy and selfish around the house?"

"I'm sure that living together will take some adjustment," said Naomi. "But I'm also sure that, if we learn to love each other, we can overcome any problems."

If only it were that easy, thought Yankl. To his chagrin, this girl seemed to have all the answers to his potential objections.

"Do you have brothers and sisters?" he asked.

"Yes, three of each. There are seven children in my family, and I'm number three. I have two older brothers who are married, each with one son, and I adore both my little nephews. Then I have three younger sisters and a brother. And you, Yankl, how many children would you like to have?"

Panic. Yankl wanted the potter's pot without the potter's wheel. Yes, he would have loved to have his own family and children, but he knew that was impossible. He forced himself back to the immediate reality.

"Well, there are three of us children. I think three is nice."

"Perhaps we can compromise at five then," said Naomi, smiling. "I like a big family."

Yankl tried to picture the impossible. He had to change the subject. He took a deep breath. "What else do you enjoy doing besides playing the piano?"

"Well, I help my mother in the kitchen. My father says my cakes are from paradise, but of course, he's biased." She laughed. "I also like to read, although it's sometimes hard to find suitable books. And you?"

I like to spend time with Velvel, he thought; but he said: "I have very little time after my day at the yeshiva. We're not encouraged to do anything else but study. Practicing the violin is all I can do."

The voice of Yankl's mother came through from the kitchen. "We're almost ready, you two. Yankl, please call in your father and Mr. Schneider from the backyard and we'll eat."

Yankl felt a mixture of sadness and relief on hearing his mother. The conversation with Naomi had gone as well as could be expected although he had clearly failed to discourage her. Yet he knew that he was playing a part, one that he would be unable to accept in real life.

The conversation flowed smoothly during the meal. It was clear that the two fathers and the two mothers had also established easy communication between them that boded well for the future. In fact, the two families seemed to have bonded, with their shared values, loving relationships and a similar standard of living. Despite his reservations, Yankl experienced a sense of comfort in this warm, friendly atmosphere, and every time he looked up, it seemed that Naomi caught his eye. The alliance of the two families was apparently taken for granted although nobody had yet asked the two young people what they thought of each other. Finally, the Schneiders took their leave, promising the Bradawkas that they would be back in touch to "make all the necessary arrangements."

After their departure, the house fell strangely silent. Mrs. Bradawka bustled about, clearing away and washing the plates and cutlery. Her husband walked up and down in the family room, humming to himself and with a smile on his face.

"Naomi's a beautiful girl, isn't she Yankl?"

"Yes, Tatteh. She's beautiful," said Yankl. "She'll make a wonderful wife."

"She'll make *you* a wonderful wife," his mother interjected from her place at the kitchen sink.

"Yes, Mommeh," said Yankl lamely. Reality suddenly flooded back.

"So," said his father, "can I tell the Schneiders that we're happy with the arrangement? Can I talk to them about setting a date?"

Yankl paused before giving his consent. "Yes, Tatteh. You can talk to them." He suddenly felt a wave of exhaustion sweep over him. "I'm very tired. I think I'll go to bed."

Mrs. Bradawka dried her hands on a towel. "Come here, Yankl," she said walking up to her son and putting her arms around him. "I knew you would eventually make us happy." She kissed his cheek.

"Yes, Mommeh. Good night. Good night, Tatteh." He slowly climbed the stairs to his room. He closed the door and fell heavily onto his bed. He could no longer think straight. The idea of marrying this girl and having a family was a wonderful prospect. Yet the idea of producing a family was something beyond his imagination. It could never happen. In his mind's eye, he saw himself in bed with Velvel on one side, Naomi on the other. He wanted so much to love Naomi, to embrace her and hold her in his arms. But with Velvel, he wanted to make passionate love, giving and receiving stimulation with his entire body and soul. He realized, the positions should be reversed: he should want to embrace Velvel and make love to Naomi. If only he could switch his emotions and his desire from one to the other. His *yetzer horah,* his evil inclination, in this case, his sexual drive needed to be spun around, from men to women. But that was impossible. With an effort, he decided to stop thinking about it. He undressed and climbed into bed. His last thought before falling into a fitful sleep was that somehow, with God's help, the situation would resolve itself.

"I remember," I mused, "When I was fifteen years old, my father insisted that I make contact with a girl, Joanne Brown. I had been to her birthday party when we were both nine years old and came home saying that she was nice. For all those years, my parents had cherished my one positive comment about a member of the opposite sex!"

"What did your father want you to do?" asked Yankl.

"How can I explain? In the world I live in, we have the telephone, a machine that enables us to talk to each other from a distance. My father wanted me to telephone Joanne and ask her to go out with me, perhaps for a walk or for a cup of tea in a restaurant."

Any attempt I might have made to describe a cinema outing to Yankl would have been too complicated. "So I telephoned her."

"What happened?"

"Well, I was terrified. Of course, I didn't want to go out with her or any other girl and then have to pretend that I wanted to see her again. Anyway, I telephoned her. She was very flattered that I showed interest in her, but, she said, she was already going out with another boy in my school."

"Were you relieved?"

"Not only was I relieved, I was deliriously happy. I whooped around the house expressing my delight. My parents had no idea why I rejoiced in such rejection. And there was no way I could explain it to them."

Yankl and I smiled at each other, enjoying the shared memory.

Chapter 12

A few days later, Leah Bradawka went to see Hannah Schneider and discovered that Naomi had been delighted with her son. The wedding day was set for one month later and the entire community would be invited to celebrate with the two families. Although the young couple could live with one or other of their parents, both mothers realized that if they were to become young grandmothers, the newlyweds should have a place of their own. Leah Bradawka and Hannah Schneider promised to make inquiries in order to find accommodation for their children, nothing too big until they had a family that required more space.

It transpired, however, that it was Yankl's father, the butcher, who discovered a place for the new bride and groom to live in. It was a Thursday, the day when most of the women in the Jewish community purchased their meat for the Sabbath.

"Good day, Mrs. Dobinski." Mr. Bradawka greeted one of his regular customers. "I have great news for you today."

"So, you're finally dropping your prices, Mr. Bradawka. That *is* good news." Mrs. Dobinski was known for her penny-pinching ways and her lashing tongue.

"Better than that, Mrs. Dobinski. It's about my son, Yankl. He's getting married."

"Oh, is that all?"

Mendl Bradawka ignored her lack of interest.

"Yes, to a lovely girl, the Schneider girl. It's a match made in heaven."

"Mazel tov, Mr. Bradawka. I'll have a pound of minced beef."

"The wedding will be in the fall, a few days before our New Year, *Rosh Hashonahh*."

"So, am I invited to the *chassana*? Are *we* invited to the wedding, me and my Feivel?" asked Mrs. Dobinski, eager to obtain the most for nothing from the man whom she considered robbed her mercilessly on a weekly basis.

"Of course, Mrs. Dobinski. You and your husband."

Warming slightly to this unaccustomed generosity, she said: "And where will the young couple live? With you and your wife?"

"We prefer not. We're looking for a place for them to live on their own."

"Hmm," pondered Mrs. Dobinski. "I think I heard of a place the other day. I met Mrs. Fogel on the street, and she was telling me that the widow, Mrs. Lipski, is planning to join her children in Warsaw. You know, Mrs. Lipski – she lives at the end of the shtetl, near the road out. She has a nice place, but small. Perhaps your children could take over her place."

"Excellent, excellent!" was the enthusiastic response. "I'll have my wife visit Mrs. Lipski as soon as possible."

That night, Mendl Bradawka told his wife about his find, and the next day, Leah walked to the edge of the shtetl to visit Mrs. Lipski. The house shone. Mrs. Lipski was not a rich woman, but everything in her house, from the samovar to the sink, glowed with the results of her efforts to keep the place clean. And the efforts she had to make were gargantuan. Almost crippled by osteoporosis, Clara Lipski, a short woman, was bent over, giving her the appearance of a benign gnome. She smiled as Leah Bradawka entered her tidy home.

"Welcome to my humble home, Mrs. Bradawka," she said warmly. "It will be hard to leave it, but I'm going to live in Warsaw with my children while I can still enjoy my grandchildren. I have nobody left here, so your children can just take over the rent and enjoy my home until they need more space for their family."

The house was small, just two rooms, a family room and a bedroom. There was also a small backyard where Yankl would be able to grow some vegetables. Leah Bradawka was enchanted by it.

"When are you moving to Warsaw?"

"I'm hoping to go in two weeks. I'd leave all the furniture. It's old but it's still comfortable, and I won't need anything when I live with my children. I'll even leave all my kitchen plates, pots and cutlery. It can be my wedding present to them. The young couple could just move in with their clothes."

"You are very generous," said Mrs. Bradawka. The house was like a sign from heaven. It was perfect. How could the marriage fail with a gem of a house like this one? It would serve nicely for a year or two. It would even be large enough to accommodate their first child, her first grandchild. Leah Bradawka took a moment to fantasize about dandling her first grandson on her knees. But what if it were a girl? That would still be acceptable, she thought.

"Mrs. Lipski, your house will be perfect for my son and his bride. I'll tell Yankl about it and he'll probably want to come and see it for himself. I think that would only be fair. To me, though, your home seems ideal."

When she arrived home, Leah Bradawka told Yankl about her find. He seemed strangely unenthusiastic.

"Alright, Mommeh, I'll go and take a look at it. I'm sure if you like it, it will be what we're looking for. I'll call on Mrs. Lipski tomorrow."

Yankl felt like a condemned man, his wedding day being the day his sentence would begin. As his parents' excitement at the prospect of their only son's wedding grew, so did his anxiety at the trap closing in upon him. Nightmares plagued his sleep, reflecting the imminent crisis he would have to face. Yet through it all, he functioned normally at the study hall and at home, forcing himself not to betray his real feelings. The only indication of his anguish was in his music. He could not bring himself to play the happy melodies that he and Velvel had loved so much. Every note that he produced on his violin was in a minor key, slow and mournful. On hearing his playing, his mother willfully blocked out any thought that Yankl might be unhappy. Tatteh did not even notice it.

Yankl went to visit Mrs. Lipski. Objectively, he could see that the house and its contents would be ideal for him and for Naomi.

"Mrs. Lipski, this is most kind of you. I do not know how to thank you for your generosity."

"Yankl, your happiness, yours and Naomi's will be my reward. I know I will be leaving the house in good hands. I had so much happiness here with my poor husband and the children, I wish you as much joy as we had. Wait, I'll go and pick some fresh vegetables for your dear mother."

Mrs. Lipski went out to the backyard to fetch her small gift for the Bradawka household. Yankl remained in the family room. He sat down in one of the two armchairs and closed his eyes. He imagined the future, just a few short weeks away. Naomi, sitting in the other armchair, her eyes red with crying, twisting a kerchief in her hands, her beautiful face distorted with grief and regret. Yankl opened his eyes. He could not bear to do this to her. She was completely innocent and should not have to suffer because of him. In his own way, he had fallen in love with that beautiful girl, but it was a love without desire. Physically entering her would be to defile that love, to desecrate both her and himself. It was a situation he must avert at all costs.

"Did your parents ever try to marry you off?" Yankl asked me.

"Yes. I remember going to some family wedding where my mother was introduced to an attractive, blonde, young woman. She was a dentist and very eligible. My mother evidently fantasized about her as a daughter-in-law and tried to force me into telephoning her to ask her out."

"How old were you then?"

"I was about 22, old enough to be able to say that I was not interested and to stand by my decision. But my mother was terribly disappointed."

"Did your parents suspect that you were not attracted to women, not to any woman?"

"Not at that time. They had no idea that someone could be attracted to a person of his own sex. It was something they could not imagine."

Chapter 13

Yankl plodded home, carrying Mrs. Lipski's vegetables and brooding about this mismatched marriage. He could not tell his parents that he did not want to marry. They would never understand. There was only one solution to the situation: he would have to remove himself from it. He contemplated a short marriage followed by a divorce; but that would seem inexplicable to others. Some of the blame for the failed alliance would inevitably fall upon Naomi and she would be considered as soiled goods, a label that Yankl considered unfair and intolerable. He would have to disappear before the ceremony.

As the enormity of his decision took hold, he came to a halt. His legs became paralyzed and his entire body became a dead weight, immovable. Recovering slightly, he staggered to a low wall at the roadside and slumped onto it, placing the vegetables by his side. He stared, unseeing around him.

The foliage on the tall trees bordering the shtetl was in full leaf. Summertime was at its peak. Soon, the shades of green would change to reds, yellows and browns, a presage of the winter to come in a few weeks. As Yankl emerged from the shock of his decision, he became aware of his surroundings, a humble human being caught up in circumstances whirling out of control. Yet to some extent he could take control of his own destiny.

Yankl pictured his future unfolding as an everlasting winter – cold, bleak and lonely. He would find himself without his family, his loving parents and his beautiful little sisters. He thought of the intense pain that he would cause them – not only his own family but Naomi and her family, too. But the pain would be short-lived and the alternative was unthinkable. If he stayed, the pain would start small and grow like an avalanche to crush them all, causing long-term harm to everyone involved. By moving on, as he planned to do, the scandal would be laid at his door alone, leaving those around him, the injured parties, blameless. He would sacrifice his own future for the lesser distress of his family and his betrothed.

He recalled similar situations. His great uncle Aaron, who had fled to America. Nobody in the family ever discussed Uncle Aaron. He had left the shtetl at the early age of seventeen, in time to avoid his own parents' matchmaking designs. And it was they who had paid his passage, having listened to his constant pleas to go to America since his tenth birthday. Aaron's occasional letters recounting his financial success in the dry goods business were read and greeted with a shrug and a sigh, as if he had been born with some physical disability. "What good is the money? He's not a complete person," his mother would say, "all alone there in New York." But how could Yankl ever afford to pay for a voyage across the ocean?

Yankl next thought of poor Shmulik Belman who had ended everything. That solution was also too radical for Yankl. He had taken a vow never to commit that sin. After all, like everyone else, he had been created in God's image, and suicide – destroying God's creation – was considered a great sin, with the victim not even entitled to burial among other Jews in the cemetery. There must be other possibilities.

So what would become of him? God had given him a gift: his talent for music. That was the solution. He would travel, moving constantly from place to place, playing his violin at family parties, perhaps teaching it, and tutoring students in Torah and Talmud in different shtetls and ghettos. He would never set down roots in order to avoid the grasp of mothers eager to marry off their daughters, at least until he was over 45 years of age. By then, he would become accepted as a confirmed bachelor. It would be a desolate existence, but nobody would be hurt except himself.

From his seat on the wall, he looked around. He noticed the small houses, the shul and the study hall. He burned them into his memory. This was the place where he had been born and raised, and where he and Velvel had met and discovered each other. It was a memory that he would treasure and from which he would draw strength. Meanwhile, he must leave no grounds for suspicion of his intentions. Let them proceed with planning the wedding. He would not be there to participate, and Naomi would be free to marry someone else, a man who could make her truly happy and give her the children she desired so much.

The wedding date was set for a Thursday in late September, shortly before the arrival of the High Holidays, the Jewish New Year and *Yom Kippur*, the Day of Atonement, a full day of fasting and the holiest days in the Jewish calendar. Yankl would pray elsewhere, repenting for the terrible pain he had caused, but in another way, proud that he had been able to summon the courage to face reality and avoid even greater tragedy.

He could not disappear, however, without a word of explanation to the people he loved. He would leave a note for his parents and another for Naomi. In no way should she blame herself for his flight from their planned marriage. He determined to draft the letters as soon as he could. They would not be easy to compose.

He arrived home and gave Mrs. Lipski's vegetables to his mother.

"Yankl, you look so pale. Is anything wrong? Do you feel well?"

"I'm alright, Mommeh. My stomach feels a bit queasy. It may be something I ate."

Leah Bradawka busied herself putting the vegetables away.

"How kind of Mrs. Lipski," she said, her attention distracted from Yankl. "It is really so good of her to pass her house on to you and Naomi. You see, everything is working out for the best." As she chattered on, Yankl's insides tightened like a vice.

"I'm going up to play some music, Mommeh." He went upstairs to his room. He could confess his feelings to nobody, but he could still express them through his music. Yet, he thought, I must give no grounds for suspicion. So he first played a happy melody, *lecha dodi,* the congregational hymn sung on Friday evenings welcoming the Sabbath, and followed it with a sad one, the cantorial solo, sung when replacing the Torah scroll in the Holy Ark in shul, which reflected his true feelings. Appropriately, the final words in that soulful piece – renew our days as of old – brought to mind the wonderful times he had spent with Velvel.

Leah Bradawka paused in her dinner preparations to listen to her son's performance. The lilting tune of his first piece reassured her that Yankl was happy. Then came the second, the minor key and the aching emotion transferred from Yankl's mind to the strings arousing an unknown dread in his mother.

"Ach," she said aloud, "why tempt Providence? Why should I worry? She's a beautiful girl. He seems happy, if a bit nervous. But that's normal." She returned to her kitchen duties, trying to push the trepidation out of her mind.

Yankl realized that he would have to muster all his strength to act out his part, and that might prove more difficult on a day-to-day basis than actually leaving. A groom was supposed to look happy at the prospect of marriage, especially marriage to a young woman as beautiful and intelligent as Naomi. Nevertheless, marriage was a major step, and grooms had been known to be more than a little nervous. Starting to share one's life with a complete stranger, and a woman at that, was good enough reason to experience butterflies in one's stomach and to lose any appetite for food. Yankl hoped that some of his anxiety could be explained by a groom's nerves, especially in the eyes of his parents who had been made well aware of his relationship with Velvel.

Various practical arrangements had to be made. Mrs. Lipski was to leave her small house ten days before the wedding, and Yankl and Naomi could install their personal effects there soon after she left. Naomi's brothers would move her clothes from their parents' home to Mrs. Lipski's house, and Yankl would carry over his clothing, as well as his precious violin, on the Monday, three days before the nuptials.

A major challenge would occur on the Sabbath prior to the wedding. On that Sabbath, it was the custom for a groom to be called to make a blessing on the final section of the weekly Torah reading in the synagogue, and then chant a section from one of the books of prophets. This Yankl would have to do. The ritual, a signal honor, was called an *aufruf*.

Normally, Yankl could accept such an assignment with equanimity, but the significance of the occasion, especially knowing that his time in the community was limited, made him extremely apprehensive. In addition, following the service, the entire congregation would flock around him to wish him the traditional words of congratulation, mazel tov, on his forthcoming wedding. He would then have to smile and acknowledge their good wishes gracefully. But the thought of his ultimate action – Naomi's future happiness without him as part of it – would give him strength.

First, he had to compose his two farewell notes. That night he smuggled a quill pen, ink and paper up to his room. By the light of his oil lamp, he sat down on his narrow bed, and using a piece of board as a support for the paper, he reflected on what he wanted to say. Nausea overcame him as he realized what he was about to do. He was ending his current way of life in exchange for exile and the unknown. Why not just go through with it – marry Naomi and suffer the consequences? Suddenly, Velvel's smiling eyes flashed before his eyes. "No," Yankl whispered to himself, "I cannot do this. I must escape."

Cymbals clashed in his head as he stared at the blank page. He lay down on his back on the bed, eyes shut tightly, his hands to his temples. How could he do this to the parents who had nurtured him, nourished him and hoped so much for him from birth? Then the voice of reality cut in: how could he stay? How could he even contemplate the unhappiness he would cause Naomi, her parents and his own parents? He had to write what he felt. He sat up and put pen to paper.

My dear Mommeh, My dear Tatteh:

This is the most difficult thing I have had to do in my life. Let me start by saying I love you both, as I know you love me. You have always wanted the best for me in every way, from the material to the spiritual, and I want to thank you so much for everything that you have done for me.

What I am going to do, what I will have done by the time you read these lines, will be extremely painful for us all. But I believe with all the conviction in my soul that I am doing the right thing. I am leaving you all, my home and my future in Rypin.

Perhaps you already suspect the reason: I cannot marry Naomi. Although she is a beautiful young woman and would make an ideal wife for me and a wonderful daughter-in-law for you, I cannot marry her. In fact, I will never marry.

I was born with no physical desire for women, none at all. And yet I have enough regard for Naomi not to impose a loveless marriage on her. I could only offer her companionship, nothing more – a childless arrangement, but that is not enough for a girl yearning to be a mother. Our wedding would be a charade, a show. Everyone would be thinking of our future happiness, but it could never be.

I have been cursed with this condition and I beg for your understanding. I cannot be a person I am not. I cannot be the person you want me to be. By leaving I will avoid causing you all the unspoken torment that would inevitably occur if I stayed.

I know that you will find this difficult to understand. Even if we talked about it, the situation would not be resolved. I ask only one thing of you: even if my behavior seems to be irrational and hurtful, please do not stop loving me and praying for me, as I shall pray for you. All I wish is that Esther and Rivka will give you the happiness that I am unable to provide.

I will write to you and can only hope that, one day, you will be able to understand and forgive me for the pain I am causing."

Yankl reread the letter, his eyes glistening with tears. Then, holding the pen as if it were a dead weight, he signed it:

Your loving son,
Yankl.

He rested his head on his hands, envisioning his mother's sobs and his father's despair. How would they face their loss? How would they explain this to the community? An unreasoned impulse, a mental seizure, a nervous breakdown? Musicians were sensitive creatures with abnormal reactions. But, at least, the blame would not fall upon his parents or on Naomi; only upon him.

Next he had to write a note to Naomi, his betrothed. Although easier to compose, his words would cause almost as much heartbreak. Naomi's immediate dreams would be shattered, but her future would be secure, and that was all that mattered. His pen touched the paper and he wrote.

Dear Naomi:

This note will come as a shock to you, one that I would sincerely wish to avoid. But that is impossible.

I cannot marry you. Please believe me when I say that this is no fault of yours. You are a beautiful and intelligent young woman for whom I have every respect. No, if there is blame to be cast, I am the one who should bear it.

I have an incurable disease that prevents me from getting married. I cannot be the husband you would want me to be, and I do not wish to cause you everlasting pain, which would be your fate if you married me. If ever there were a woman I could marry, you would be the one. But you could never be happy with me.

Do not blame my parents for not having revealed my condition to you before. They were completely ignorant of it and only now have I made them aware of it.

I am leaving Rypin. I must make my future elsewhere.

Please forgive me if you can. All I wish for you is happiness with a husband who will love you as you deserve, provide for your needs and give you the fulfillment you desire.

Yankl

It was Thursday, just one week before the planned wedding day. This time next week, he was expected to consummate his marriage with the beautiful Naomi. But this time next week, he would be far from home, reflecting on what might have been and living the inevitable loneliness the future held in store for him. He hid the letters between his shirts in a drawer and went to bed, exhausted and shivering with fear at the consequences of his action.

Chapter 14

The next morning, after Mendl had left for the shop and Yankl for the yeshiva, Leah bustled about the house preparing food for the last shabbes her son would be spending as a single man under her roof. Everything would turn out for the best. In one week, her son would be married and she would then have another daughter, Naomi, with whom to chat and share confidences. Her thoughts and actions were interrupted by a knock on the front door. A young lad stood there.

"Good morning," he said. "I'm from the inn. I have a letter for you. I mean for Yankl."

Leah took the letter and sat down at the table, staring at it. Who could have sent a letter to her son, who never received letters? What should she do with it? She stared at it for a few moments. The letter must have been sent by Velvel, she realized, her heart in her mouth. Velvel had written to him. Leah decided to open the letter and read it.

My very dear Yankl, she read. She looked away from the letter. Did she have the right to do this? A letter between lovers, albeit both male? Yes. She answered her own question. It could do Yankl no good to hear from a lover whom he would never see again. She read on.

> *How could they have done this to us? How could they destroy what we had? I miss you terribly. My own pain at losing you fades only when I think of yours. I am here in Vilna...*

Leah's eyes left the page. So Velvel had not been sent to Warsaw, she thought. Had it been the rabbi who started this rumor to prevent Yankl from trying to trace his lover? She returned to her reading. What a mean ruse!

> *I try to think of the words of Talmud I study every day. But my mind is elsewhere. It is with you and the wonderful times we spent together. Your smile and your music. Your mind and your body. Your caring for me. Will we ever recapture those times?*
>
> *They will not let us. I sometimes wonder if they realize the depth of their own cruelty. Were we harming them? Yankl, all I pray for is that you may read these lines and answer me. Please tell me that, one day we may meet again. There will never be another 'Yankl' in my life. Perhaps if we both pray for each other, God will answer our prayers.*
>
> *I will always love you.*
>
> *Velvel*

Leah's eyes were damp. She could not doubt the sincerity of Velvel's feelings for her son. She wondered whether, at another time and in another place, such a union would ever be permitted. However, there and then it could never be. Leah took the letter, crossed the room to the stove and threw it in. She watched it burn. Yankl could not be allowed to see it and be diverted from the path he had agreed to follow. She decided to try and put the letter out of her mind.

"Strange," I said. "My own parents also discovered the way I felt through a letter, but it was a copy of a letter I myself sent."

"Tell me about it," said Yankl.

"I had written a letter, a love letter, to a male friend of mine and had kept a copy of it. I left the copy in the pocket of one of my jackets.

My mother decided to send the jacket to the cleaners. Let me explain: when it comes to small articles of clothing, we have machines at home to wash them. But we take larger items to a professional laundry. My mother wanted to be sure that the pockets were empty before the jacket was cleaned, and that's how she discovered the letter."

"So then what happened?"

"The next day, my father confronted me with the letter and asked whether I was attracted to men. By then, I was financially independent – I was 23 years old – and I saw no reason to deny it. But the consequences were dramatic." I paused, remembering the pain I had caused.

"My parents and I had a serious conversation. My father insisted on sending me to see a doctor who specializes in treating mental disorders, what we call a psychiatrist, although I told him that I, myself, had already consulted four of them, with no positive results. But to satisfy him, I agreed to attend a meeting with what my father called 'the best physician in the land.'"

"Did he do you any good?" asked Yankl, fascinated.

"No, but he was honest. He said he could treat me, with no promise of success, and that I would have to visit him five times a week, and give up any male friends I had made.

"That was not good enough for me, or for my father. The doctor's fees were very high, and he could not guarantee success. In addition, I had put a great deal of time and effort into establishing a few friendships that I would definitely not give up. So my father decided to accept the inevitable."

"What was the inevitable?"

"When you cannot change a situation, you either fight it or accept it and adapt to it. My father, of blessed memory, was a wise man. He knew that I had no choice in the matter so he read books about my condition and realized that nothing was really wrong with me. It's just a matter of being attracted to men rather than to women. In fact, today, we realize that some women also are attracted to other women rather than to men."

"And how did your mother accept the situation?"

"She could not share my father's attitude. For her, fear of rejection by friends and family because of my inability to marry and my attraction to men paralyzed her. She rejected me because she was afraid that she, herself, would be rejected, and her life was clouded by blaming herself for the way I felt. She also thought I could choose to change. Of course, I would have done anything to change, but there was no choice. My father and I learned to live with the person I was and I believe he was actually proud of me. My mother could never face my reality. A real tragedy."

"I'm sorry," said Yankl.

"Ultimately, it was her decision over which I had no control. I could certainly not change my own nature, nor could I change hers. She was a victim of what she saw as the convention of the day."

Chapter 15

The last Sabbath evening meal before the wedding was a trial for Yankl. His parents' evident happiness sent daggers through his heart. Again, he questioned the need for the pain and disappointment he would cause them by running away. All their hopes and expectations for their only son would be dashed by his disappearance. The family name would be extinguished with him. Once more, he tried to imagine lying next to Naomi on his wedding night, and the prospect made his stomach churn. There really was no choice. He put on a brave face.

"So, Yankl, your last shabbes meal as a single man under the family roof. You must be so excited," said his father.

"Yes, Tatteh, I am," replied Yankl, forcing a smile. "On Monday I'll move my things into the house."

"I'll put the suitcase in your room after shabbes," said Leah Bradawka. "I can even help you pack."

"No, Mommeh, that really won't be necessary." Yankl panicked mentally as he imagined his mother sorting through his shirts and finding his goodbye letters. "I'll pack on Sunday and take my things to the house on Monday."

Monday. A shudder ran through his body at the thought that, in three days his entire life in Rypin would come to an end. It was like dying. The food before him would no longer be put on the table. He would have nobody to depend on but himself, and he would suffer the vagaries of the outside world without any of the loving support and sustenance he had always known.

Yankl forced himself to eat. The food had no taste and he swallowed it with difficulty. That night he lay awake, dreading the pre-marriage celebration that awaited him in shul the next morning. But as is often the case, his fears were not realized. When his name was called at the end of the reading from the Torah, he focused all his attention on chanting the section from the prophets. At the conclusion of the service, he acknowledged the congratulations of family, friends and fellow-congregants, purposefully assuming that their plaudits referred to his chanting, not to his anticipated marriage.

The next day, Sunday, Yankl carefully prepared his suitcase. He packed only the clothes that he would be able to carry away from Rypin easily. He also put the money that he had earned through his music in the suitcase. He would carry his violin, the source of his future income, in his free hand and drape his overcoat over his arm. His hat, the fur *shtreimel* that he wore on shabbes, was attached to the outside of the suitcase. The farewell notes he had written were placed in his overcoat pocket so that, on arriving at what would have been his new home, he could easily extract them and leave them on the kitchen table. He imagined himself as a warrior going off to war. He had to maintain his composure so as not to alarm his family, in spite of feeling sick with fear. This was a campaign for him to claim his life and save his family from drawn-out pain and possible shame. He had to believe that he had chosen the best and only path to follow.

Monday dawned. As usual, his father left early for the butcher's shop. Yankl rose. It was as if he could see himself going through all the motions of washing and dressing from a bird's eye view. He acted automatically. He placed his phylacteries, his *tefillin,* on his arm and head but was unable to pray. Why had God cursed him with this condition? Why did he have to end the life he had known? There were no answers. He just had to deal with the situation as he thought best.

He ate a light breakfast, wondering where his next meal would come from. There was no conversation with his mother, both she and he already missing each other. Leah Bradawka thought her son was just moving to the other side of the shtetl. Yankl knew that he was moving out of her life. He left the table.

"It's as though I'm losing you," said the mother, wiping away a tear.

"Mommeleh, you'll never lose me," said the son, using the diminutive in addressing his mother. His concern for her peace of mind was greater than his urge to disguise his own despair. "I'll be living only a few minutes away" he lied, "and we'll be able to see each other often." He held her in his arms and kissed her cheek.

Esther and Rivka were playing on the floor.

"Come here little sisters," said Yankl, "and see your big brother off." The two little girls ran to him and, with some effort, he lifted them one in each arm, so that they could embrace him before he set off. It was too much for him. He had been like a second father to the girls. Tears flowed down his cheeks and it was his mother's turn to comfort him.

"Yankl, Yankl, why the tears? This is a moment of joy. This is what we've hoped and prayed for, for so long. Come, take your things and go, and we'll all be together again later."

Yankl put the two little girls down. "You're right, Mommeh. We'll all be together again later."

He took the suitcase with his hat, the violin and coat and went through the door without looking back, tears still streaming from his eyes.

He hardly felt the weight of the suitcase. At the end of the street, he wiped his eyes with a kerchief, looked back once, and trudged on to Mrs. Lipski's house. It would never be his. It would never be theirs. He was thankful that it was located on the outskirts of the shtetl. Nobody need see him walk on and away.

He entered the house, wondering who would next occupy it. In his mind's eye, he saw his parents or Naomi discovering his notes, and immediately cast aside the thought. Such imaginings could do no good. He took out the notes and looked at them. He kissed them, first his parents', then Naomi's, and placed them prominently on the kitchen table.

Nearby were several suitcases that Naomi's brothers had moved into the house for her. Yankl looked at them. They would not remain in the house for much longer. Her suitcases and his notes. An incompatible combination.

From this moment on, his concerns had to be only for himself. He would be his own father, his own mother, his own son. The society into which he had been born had refused to acknowledge the person he was and had forced him, in turn, to reject it. But Yankl realized that he need not, as a consequence, reject his entire heritage. He still believed in a benevolent God, one to whom he could turn in times of trouble, and whom he could thank for good fortune. On reflection, he was determined to make the most of his life despite the lack of a family. He had a wonderful gift, his music, that he could share with others to lighten the load of their lives. He would not allow the awful experience he was going through to crush him indefinitely.

Yankl took out his *siddur,* his prayer book, and sat down at the table. He turned to the page for the Wayfarer's Prayer, recited by travelers before setting out on any potentially dangerous journey. It was almost as if the words had been composed especially for him.

> *And Yaacov (Hebrew for Yankl) continued his journey and was met by God's angels... God sent an angel before him to guide him on his way and to bring him to the place that God had prepared for him. May God bless you and keep you; may His face shine upon you and may He be gracious to you; may He turn his face to you and give you peace.*
>
> *You, O Lord, are my protection. You will keep trouble far from me, You will surround me with melodies of deliverance.*

Yankl closed his eyes and prayed earnestly for the fortitude to withstand the loneliness that he had never known in the past, but which would be the hallmark of his future life.

He stood, took some money out of his suitcase, closed it and left the house carrying it in his hand. He closed the door carefully behind him and began his journey away from Rypin.

Strangely, he was calm. He had done it. He was now his own person and the pilot of his own destiny. But he wanted an even more radical break with his past identity. He found it in his name. He would change his name. The patriarchs of the Jewish people who had changed their names sprang to mind – Abram who had become Abraham, Jacob who had become Israel after wrestling with the angel, and Hosea who had become Joshua. So who was the hero he most admired in Jewish history? The name immediately flashed before his eyes: Jonathan. Jonathan, the biblical character whom the future King David had loved with "a love greater than that for a woman." Jonathan who had loved David, the youth with a ruddy complexion like Velvel's, "as his own soul." From now on, he would be known as Jonathan. And to complete the transformation, he would change his family name, too. Something like Bradawka but shorter. Brodski. Jonathan Brodski. He would be Jonathan Brodski, the violinist, the Jewish fiddler, the Torah and Talmud tutor. That was how he would introduce himself.

The houses tapered off and the forest closed in on the road. Jonathan walked for an hour and then rested, his back against a tree. He remembered how he had sat in that position with Velvel, Velvel's head upon his lap, his beautiful eyes looking up into Yankl's. Jonathan closed his eyes, remembering.

The sound of wooden wheels on the rough road awakened him. It was the carter, traveling from Rypin to the next shtetl with parcels and letters to deliver. Jonathan hailed him, climbed onto the cart and left Rypin, never to return.

"I remember when I decided to leave London, where I was born, and emigrate to Canada. But, I'm sure you'll understand, Jonathan" – I felt it only polite to use the new name Yankl had chosen for himself – "several factors in my life came together to leave me little choice."

"And what were they?" Jonathan asked.

"First, my position at work – I was unable to make progress in my job and I could not find a better place to work. Then I was in a relationship with another man, but I could not return his affection. Emigration would provide a logical escape. Finally, I wanted to travel before I was 30. But the break was as difficult for me as yours was for you."

"In what way?"

"Well, when you moved to Poznan, you remained basically within the same culture although I know that there was a strong Prussian influence there. I moved from London, one of the largest cities in the world with a rich cultural life that I enjoyed to the full, to Vancouver, a much smaller city on the west coast of Canada, on the Pacific Ocean, with little cultural activity. Later, when employment became problematic there, I decided to travel back to Montreal, halfway home to London, where my mother's cousins lived. They took me in and were like surrogate parents to me. Without them, I could not have survived in Canada. In spite of that, it took two years before I adapted to my new country."

Chapter 16

As Yankl left the family house, Leah Bradawka was filled with a sense of foreboding. Somehow, she felt, his grief at leaving her and his two sisters had been exaggerated. After all, he would be home for the evening meal, wouldn't he? After depositing his clothes and violin at Mrs. Lipski's house, he was supposed to return to the study hall, spend the day there and come home, as usual. She tried to dismiss her uneasiness, but the thought kept nagging at her. What if he could not bring himself to go through with this marriage? In the last few days, he had been unusually quiet, not excited as she would have expected a young groom to be. He had seemed resigned to a fate chosen for him by others. Was that normal? What if he decided to make a gesture of total defiance and do away with himself?

She panicked. She decided to go to the study hall to check that Yankl was there and that nothing was amiss. Although summer was not yet over, there was a chill in the air. Leah threw a shawl over her shoulders and went next door to Mrs. Chaskel's house to ask her if she could leave her young daughters with her while she herself ran some errands, a convenient excuse that masked her real reason.

"With pleasure," said Mrs. Chaskel. Her own young boys were out of the house all day, either at the cheder or in the study hall, and she enjoyed having the two Bradawka girls as company while she busied herself with the household chores.

Having dropped off the children, Leah walked briskly to the study hall. As a woman, she was not allowed inside – her presence would have been a great distraction to the young men. She stopped a man who was passing by and asked him if he would kindly step inside and ask Yankl Bradawka to come out for a word with his mother. The man disappeared inside. As the minutes passed, Leah's anxiety grew. What was keeping him? All he had to do was ask the *shammes,* the man in charge of minor study hall details, to go to Yankl's desk and ask him to come out. Nothing happened. The minutes passed. Leah paced up and down the boardwalk outside the study hall. At last the man emerged.

"He's not there," he said.

"Not there?" All her fears were being realized. "Are you sure?"

"He was not at his desk and has not appeared this morning. Is everything all right? Are you all right?"

"Yes, yes. I'm all right," said Leah distractedly. "Thank you. It's probably nothing. Thank you for your help."

Leah's steps led her like a clockwork toy back toward her house. But where could he be? The last place he had intended to go was Mrs. Lipski's house. Perhaps he was still there. She changed direction and half walked, half ran to the end of the shtetl toward what was to be her son's future home. As she hurried round a corner she stumbled and almost fell. She leaned against the wall of a house for support as tears of fear welled up in her eyes. Afraid of arousing the curiosity of passers-by, she edged into a nearby alley.

With her back to the wall she looked heavenward and whispered, "*Gott im Himmel,* God in Heaven, keep him safe." She imagined his lifeless body swinging from a branch, like that of poor Shmulik, or drifting down the river, or worst of all, her beautiful son smashed on the ground after a leap from a high place. She shook her head from side to side as if plagued by a virulent insect, trying to dash the horrific images from her head. "I must find him," she mumbled as she hurried on.

As she reached Mrs. Lipski's old house, she stood outside for a moment, dreading what she might find inside. She muttered another prayer as she pushed open the door.

Her first glance into the room fell upon suitcases. Breathing a sigh of relief, she entered the room. There was no sign of Yankl. Perhaps he had decided to play truant and go for a walk in the nearby forest. She looked for his violin and, failing to find it, she thought that he had taken it with him. Then she looked back at the suitcases. She did not recognize them, nor could she see the one Yankl had taken with him that morning. Yes, she thought, they must be Naomi's. But where was Yankl's?

She sat down in the armchair, again looking around the room. Something white on the table caught her eye. She stood. There were two notes, one addressed to Mommeh and Tatteh. Leah took the note and slumped back into the armchair, shivering with apprehension. She rested her head on the back of the chair, terrified at the prospect of what she guessed was written in the note to her and her husband. She wanted to savor these last few moments of doubt, of denial. Perhaps there was some other explanation. Perhaps her doubts and fears had been misplaced. She could delay no longer.

She unfolded the note and read:

> *My dear Mommeh, My dear Tatteh:*
>
> *This is the most difficult thing I have had to do in my life…*

When she opened her eyes, the note was on the floor beside the armchair. As if in a dream, Leah Bradawka picked it up and read her son's farewell note. Calmly, with no sense of reality, she refolded it and put it in her pocket. She rose, left the house and walked, in a trance, to her husband's butcher shop, oblivious to the greetings of one or two friends as she passed them by.

Mendl Bradawka was serving a customer as his wife pushed open the door. Two or three chairs were ranged against a wall for women waiting to be served. They were empty. Leah sank into one of them and leaned her head against the wall as tears flowed silently down her face.

The customer, preoccupied with her purchases, left without noticing Leah's distress. Not so Mendl. Alarmed, he closed the shop door and pulled down the shutter. He sat down next to his wife, and took her hand.

"Leah, my love, what is it? Tell me what's the matter?"

"We've lost our son, Tatteh," she said handing him Yankl's note.

Mendl Bradawka looked at the folded paper for a few moments, then unfolded it. He read his son's words, his cheeks becoming flushed as his anger rose like bile. He stood up, put the note in his pocket and paced back and forth across the floor of his butcher shop. Remembering the reasons for his son's forced marriage, Mendl was incapable of absorbing his son's words of love for him and his wife. All he could think of was his son's refusal to comply with his and the rabbi's decision for him to marry. Yankl had rejected them, had refused to accept their decision and had abandoned their way of life. Blinded by his anger, he hardly noticed Leah, his wife, slumped in her chair, her eyes closed and her head resting on the wall behind her.

"Yes," said Tatteh. "We've lost him." He continued to pace. "Not only have we lost him, but we are dead to him and he is dead to us."

Leah knew what was coming. She leaned forward, her elbows on her knees and her face in her hands. Sobs escaped her lips and wracked her body. Mendl's anger at his son was instantly supplanted by his love and sympathy for his wife. He sat down again next to her and put his arm across her shoulders to comfort her.

"Mommeleh, I love you. We, I and the girls love you. You will never lose us."

But, he thought, we will have to mourn our son properly. The reality of the situation struck Mendl like a hammer. He took his arm from Leah's shoulders and held his own body with both arms, rocking backward and forward, living his own grief. The couple remained in their individual blackness for several minutes.

Then Mendl's sense of betrayal returned. "Our son has rejected us and the way we live. He has refused to marry a beautiful girl, a girl whom he seemed to like. Come," he said, as he rose to take charge, "I'll take you home, and then I'll go and see Rabbi Levy. He will know exactly what is to be done."

Leah did not budge. Her eyes were still closed.

"Mendl, Mendl, what did we do to deserve this? Did we not love him enough? How could he tell us he loves us and do this to us? I don't understand. I just don't understand."

"Come, Mommeleh, we must be brave. Let me take you home. I'll ask Mrs. Chaskel to sit with you. You won't be alone."

Once again, he put his arm around her and helped her to her feet. He locked the shop door as they left and walked home, Leah leaning on her husband for support. Mendl told concerned passers-by that his wife was not feeling well – possibly something she had eaten.

Mrs. Chaskel was only too pleased to help out. She left a note at home saying where she was and came next door to the Bradawka house, bringing the two young girls with her. Mendl explained to his daughters that Mommeh was not well, and that they should let her rest quietly. Rivka and Esther were upset, but Mrs. Chaskel talked to them optimistically about their mother's imminent recovery. Leah remained on her bed in a state of shock. Mendl told his daughters and Mrs. Chaskel that he had to go back to work and that Leah was sure to be all right by the time he came home.

But Mendl Bradawka did not go back to his shop. Instead, he went straight to the study hall to see the rabbi. However, Rabbi Levy was giving a talk to a group of yeshiva students about the various interpretations of a widow's rights. Mendl had to wait until he had finished. He could not sit down. He leaned against a wall, his eyes closed trying to shut out the shock of the moment.

As the rabbi left the group, Mendl Bradawka walked up to him.

"Excuse me, rabbi," he said, "I have an emergency. May I speak with you for a few minutes?"

"Come, Reb Bradawka, we'll go into my study." The two men walked next door to the rabbi's study adjacent to the shul. They sat down.

"Rabbi, forgive me. Just give me a moment."

Mendl put his head in his hands, overcome with grief. "All our hopes… Finished… No future… Our wonderful boy…" His body heaved as he agonized.

"Mendl." Alarmed, the rabbi used his first name. "What has happened to Yankl?"

"Gone. Gone for ever. He's left us." Mendl pulled Yankl's note out of his pocket and handed it to the rabbi.

Rabbi Levy read Yankl's note. "Mendl, you know what this means." It was a statement more than a question. Mendl Bradawka nodded, too disturbed to talk.

"After what happened with that other boy, the boy he was with, you and Leah will have to say goodbye to your son forever. You will have to mourn him, to sit shiva. Yankl has refused to accept what we planned for him to help him recover from that abominable situation. He has shunned us, and he has shamed us."

Mendl let out a cry. "My family… Our name… The disgrace…"

"Listen to me, Mendl. People will understand. They won't judge you. You still have a family. A wonderful wife, two beautiful young daughters. You must be strong, for them. You will do what is necessary. You will grieve. And then you will go on with your lives. This tragedy is something you will continue to live with but it must not prevent you from living."

Mendl Bradawka swayed backward and forward in his chair. Yesterday he was so happy, for his son and for himself. For Leah, there would have been another daughter, and for the girls, an older sister. Today, his world had disintegrated.

"Mendl." Rabbi Levy brought Mendl back to reality. "We must begin the process immediately. In an hour, we will say the afternoon and evening prayers here in the study hall. You will join us. You will say the prayer for the dead, the Kaddish, with us. And then we will walk home together and you will begin to sit shiva. You and Leah. Your friends and family will come and visit you. They will support you. And, believe me, Mendl, with God's help, you will get through this."

Mendl Bradawka looked stunned. "But my girls, rabbi. We must first find an explanation for my girls. Yankl is no longer part of their lives and Leah and I will be sitting shiva..."

"You're right Mendl. We must cushion the blow for your girls. For the time being, we can find another reason for his disappearance. I suggest you tell the girls that Yankl had a terrible accident." The rabbi paused for a second or two. He put his hand to his eyes, praying for an inspired fabrication. "Tell them that he drowned. Tell them that his clothes were found by the river but his body must have been carried downstream by the current and disappeared. Later, when they are grown, Leah may decide to tell them the truth."

"Ay, ay ay, Rabbi, what a situation. My only son, gone. People will ask questions. They'll have to know. Even now. When they see me saying the Kaddish in the study hall they'll have to be told. But let me save what I can. Please, can you wait until this evening to bring over the low shiva chairs so that I have time to break the news to my girls?"

"Of course, Mendl. But first, we have to tear *keriya,* tear part of your clothing as a sign of your mourning. Come, stand up, say the blessing, the *brocha* on hearing of the death of a relative."

Mendl stood, his face streaked with tears as he recited: "Blessed are You, oh Lord, King of the universe, the true judge."

Rabbi Levy took a razor from his desk drawer and made a slight nick in the collar of Mendl's shirt. Mendl reached up and tore it further, leaving an open gash in the fabric.

"Come let us go in and pray, and may God comfort you among others in mourning for Zion and Jerusalem." His final phrase was the customary greeting of sympathy extended to the bereaved.

Chapter 17

Mendl Bradawka withstood the surprised stares of the young men in the study hall as he recited the Kaddish. He left without a word as soon as the service concluded, so it fell to Rabbi Levy to explain to his students why Mendl was saying Kaddish. Rabbi Levy told the truth as the youths clustered around him, full of questions.

"Mendl Bradawka is saying kaddish for Yankl his son who has run away. He decided that he didn't want to marry, ever. So this is the result. I will not go into the details. Just accept the fact that Mr. Bradawka has to be a mourner, an *ovel,* and we will all give him and his family the support that they need."

A buzz rose from the students gathered before the rabbi. Yankl was one of the most talented students among them. "How could he have spurned such a wonderful opportunity?" they whispered to each other. Marriage was one of the greatest gifts God bestowed on man, the source of intense happiness. The young men's speculation was cut short.

"Gentlemen, there is nothing further to discuss," said the rabbi. "The matter is now closed."

Mendl staggered home, seeming intoxicated. His head spun with sorrow as if struck by a sudden debilitating disease. Yet through the mist of his misfortune, he reasoned with himself: this is not my tragedy alone. I have to be strong for Leah and my girls. They are all I have left and they are very precious to me. God, give me the strength to give them the courage to continue with their lives as best they can. And God, give me the strength to continue with mine.

When Mendl reached his home, the lamps were lit but the house was quiet. No clatter of dishes, no girlish laughter, no conversation. He entered the house. Mrs. Chaskel was reading to the girls from the Book of Ruth. Leah was still lying on the bed, her right arm over her forehead.

"Mrs. Chaskel," he said, "I want to thank you for helping out. I can take care of the girls now."

Mrs. Chaskel said: "I've warmed up some soup for you all on the stove, and there's some bread and fruit in the pantry. Make sure your wife eats something. She must keep up her strength. And please call upon me, Mr. Bradawka if there's anything you need. Anything at all."

"Thank you again, so much, Mrs. Chaskel."

Their good neighbor left the house to return to her own family, casting a last anxious look toward the ailing Leah Bradawka, Mendl set cutlery on the table for himself and the girls.

"Come Esther, come Rivka, first we'll eat and then we'll talk and I'll tell you what's going on." He ladled out the soup into the girls' bowls, pouring very little into his own. He had completely lost his appetite. Later he would give Leah a little soup. She had to eat something.

The two girls ate in silence, sensing that something was very wrong but too young to conceive of any possible tragedy. But it was strange that Yankl had not come home. Perhaps he had somewhere else to go. When they had finished the soup and after eating some slices of apple, their father lifted them both onto his armchair. He knelt down in front of them, taking one small hand in each of his rougher palms. He took a deep breath.

"Esterel, Rivkeleh..." He used their diminutives. "Something very terrible has happened." He suppressed a sob. "It's your brother, Yankl." A tear began to flow down Esther's cheek. She was the older girl. Mendl struggled to go on.

"Tatteh, where is he?" Esther whispered. "Is he coming home?"

"*Nein*, my little darlings. He's not." Mendl let the girls' hands go and, putting his arms around them, he drew them to his chest as strangled sobs escaped his throat. He was unable to speak. In the next room, Leah, hearing her husband finally break down, rose slowly from the bed and came into the living room. She looked at her distraught family. They needed her. In turn, she knelt down by her husband, put her arms around him and the girls and gave vent to her overwhelming grief. The girls, shocked and afraid by their parents' unaccustomed display of emotion, also started to cry. For several moments, the small family was locked together in pain, holding onto each other, drawing some small comfort from their closeness, and giving some small comfort to each other.

Finally, Mendl said: "We must go on. We must go on together."

Leah lifted her two girls, sat on the armchair and cradled her daughters on her lap.

"Esterel, Rivkeleh," said Mendl, "Your brother Yankl will not be coming home. His clothes were found by the river but he was not found. He was probably swimming in the river and went out too far. We are sure he has drowned."

Leah looked at Mendl but said nothing.

"Your mother and I will have to sit shiva for him." Esther and Rivka were still crying.

"Won't he ever come back?" asked Rivka through her tears.

"No, my darling," said Tatteh. "But we must be brave and help each other. We will never forget him, but he would want us to be brave. So we must."

Leah said: "And tonight, girls, as a special treat, you'll sleep with me in my bed. Just tonight. Tatteh, please, you'll sleep here in your chair. I'll make you comfortable. Come, Esterel, Rivkeleh, I'll put you to bed."

Leah took her little daughters to wash their face and then led them into the bedroom. She undressed them and put them in her bed, next to that of her husband, for a shared bed was considered unseemly. As Leah left, their father came into the room, knelt by the bed nestling his two daughters and recited the first paragraph of the *shema,* the bedtime prayer, with them. He kissed them goodnight and left the girls to fall asleep, still disturbed by the family crisis, but somewhat comforted by being in their mother's bed.

Mendl returned to the living room. Leah sat in her armchair, staring, unseeing, straight ahead.

"Mommele, you must eat a little. I'll prepare some soup for you."

"I don't want anything," she murmured.

"For me. For the girls. Please, a little."

"A little, then, very little."

Mendl brought her a small bowl of soup. As Leah still sat motionless, Mendl fed her like a baby. She swallowed mechanically.

Shortly before the Bradawka's bedtime, Rabbi Levy and a student knocked at their door, carrying two low shiva chairs. Leah put on an old scarf in which the rabbi made a small ceremonial tear indicating her bereavement. The couple sat on the chairs, stunned at the novel experience, as once again, the rabbi and the anonymous student recited the traditional greeting to mourners before they left. For a few minutes the parents sat on the low chairs, wordless. Mendl then took Leah's hand.

"Come, my dear," he said, "let's go to bed and try to put this terrible day behind us."

Jonathan leaned forward in his chair and covered his face with his hands.

"How could I have done that to them?" He took a deep breath. "Yet how could I have avoided doing that to them?"

"Sometimes we must choose the lesser of two evils," I said. "In your heart of hearts, you know you made the right decision and saved them from even greater grief down the road. And that applies to Naomi and her family, too."

"I know," said Jonathan looking up. "But that does not make the pain or the guilt easier to bear."

BOOK 2

Chapter 1

The newly named Jonathan listened to the wheels of the cart as it traveled west away from Rypin. He knew that he should look forward to his new life rather than brood over the old. His drastic step, his refusal to be forced into a life that was not for him, had been taken. Now he had to consider his options.

His introspection was interrupted by the carter's voice. With a start, Yankl heard the name he had vowed to surrender.

"So, Yankl, you're leaving us. You're leaving town."

Yankl recognized the identity of the carter, Dov Belman, the father of Shmulik, the boy who had committed suicide. The one thing that Yankl had failed to consider in planning his escape was the fact that the driver of his means of transport would be someone with whom he had shared a crisis, the tragic death of Shmulik. Yankl noticed that the hair below the carter's cap had turned from a dark salt-and-pepper hue to pure white in the few months since his son's sad demise.

"Yes, Mr. Belman," he said, wishing that he could avoid the coming conversation.

Mr. Belman started to hum a niggun. Yankl said nothing.

Finally, Mr. Belman said: "So tell me, Yankl, what about the wedding?" The entire shtetl knew about the forthcoming wedding of the butcher's son.

Yankl did not answer immediately. Both he and Dov Belman knew why Shmulik had killed himself. Perhaps Mr. Belman would understand Yankl's predicament.

"I cannot..." Yankl spoke softly, faltering.

"You were saying? I couldn't hear you."

Yankl spoke up. "I cannot. I cannot marry."

Dov Belman hesitated. Should he pursue this conversation? Would he be prying? Then he pondered his own pain on losing his only son, his own and his wife's sense of inadequacy at failing to recognize their son's nature, their boy's change of mood after his betrothal, his real needs. Yankl, he realized, had more in common with his son, Shmulik, than was apparent. Neither of them was capable of marrying and all the pressures of community and family could do nothing to change that. Yankl, however, was taking the other option, life. He was giving up everything to be his own person. But what was he leaving behind? Dov Belman knew what his poor parents would be forced to face.

"Your parents. How will they feel about this? And the girl?"

The question tore at Yankl's heart. But anger rose to his lips.

"Do you think I have not thought about that? Do you think I want to leave? Would I willfully hurt the people most precious to me? What choice do I have?"

Dov Belman could find no answers to this stream of questions. He again started humming his niggun. What would he have wanted for his son, Shmulik, in view of the circumstances? Yankl was blessed with a portable profession. He could take his violin with him and earn a living anywhere. Shmulik had been born with no innate talent for anything. Distributing and collecting the books of Talmud in the yeshiva was the most he had been able to do. He had possessed neither the inner resources nor the self-confidence to support himself. So with a marriage already arranged, what alternative did his son have?

Dov Belman gripped the reins of his old horse more tightly and stared straight ahead as a single tear trickled down his cheek. He must not blame Yankl for leaving Rypin.

"Yankl, I'm sorry. Yes, it must have been a very difficult decision for you."

"Mr. Belman, had I stayed, I would have caused even more shame and grief than leaving. I could not do that to them. I hope you can understand." Yankl thought of Shmulik. "I'm sure you can understand," he added. Then, like a bird taking wing after a storm, a strange sense of liberation raised Yankl's spirits. For the first time since Velvel's hasty departure, Yankl had unashamedly admitted his true feelings to another human being.

Dov Belman remained silent. Then he said, with a deep sigh: "Oy, Yankl, if we could only live in another world!"

Nothing more was said. Dov Belman's thoughts churned with his deep sense of loss. Yankl, his brief feeling of elation somewhat mitigated by the carter's mention of his parents and his betrothed, turned his thoughts to contemplating an uncertain future. In a way, he himself was dying – removing himself from an intolerable existence to be reborn into a different life, one of his own choosing. Mourning his past, celebrating his future.

The cart moved slowly through the countryside. The horse drawing it was far from young. Yankl stared at the forest, preoccupied by thoughts of his parents' distress on discovering his note. The shade cast by the forest seemed to reflect his dark mood, and as the sun rose higher in the sky, humidity descended on the little vehicle like a damp blanket. Around the villages they passed through, the forest gave way to fields. Yankl gazed at the wheat and corn swaying gently in the breeze, and at the cows who barely noticed the passing cart. Chickens scampered and squawked in the yards of village houses at their approach. Not everything was dark and dank like the forest, Yankl thought. There were also fertile fields and domestic animals. The scenery was varied. Life, too, came with its ups and downs. He realized his sadness, too, would pass, and as the master of his own destiny, he could look forward to at least some good times.

Two hours later, the cart drew into Torun, a picturesque town on the Vistula River. The two men climbed down.

"Yankl, I want to wish you good luck. You are a brave young man and I know you will do well."

Yankl looked at Dov Belman and saw his own father. Dov Belman looked at Yankl and saw what his son might have been. The father and the son embraced, both with tears in their eyes.

"May you be spared further sorrow, Mr. Belman, and I wish you only *naches*, joy, from your daughters. I am glad that it was you who brought me here."

After Yankl had paid him a small sum for the trip, Dov Belman loaded some packages that were to be taken back to Rypin, turned his cart around, and with bowed head, set off on his lonely journey back home. It would be the last time Yankl would hear the name his parents had given him. From that moment on he would be his own adopted son, Jonathan.

He looked around. People were bustling about their business, but this was a small place. So where should he go? In which direction? He needed a town that was large enough for him to be relatively anonymous, one that contained a community and a yeshiva into which he could blend. His choice fell upon Poznan. The city was only two days' journey from Torun, and with his new identity, he could find work and support himself there without having his past intrude and ruin his life yet again. With some more of the money he had taken with him, he could pay for his transportation and a night's lodging in a Jewish-owned hostelry along the way. He climbed aboard the next coach to Poznan.

When night fell, he found himself in the small town of Inowroclaw where there was a Jewish-owned inn. The innkeeper was a jovial man who enjoyed meeting and chatting with the guests passing through his establishment. As the passengers climbed down from the stagecoach, he noticed Jonathan's violin case.

"So, young man," he said, "you're a musician."

"Yes, I am." Jonathan was flattered by the attention. More than that, he glimpsed the possibility of an opportunity. "And I play quite well, I'm told." He did not want to appear boastful.

"So perhaps after dinner, you'll give us a performance? My wife, you'll see, performs like a master, or should I say 'mistress' in the kitchen." He laughed at his own poor joke. "Wait till you taste her productions from the kitchen! And then, you can end our meal with a production of your own!"

It was true: the innkeeper's wife was a wizard in the kitchen and the meal she served was worthy of any festive table. *Gefilte fish,* the traditional ground and boiled fish, borscht, roast chicken with vegetables and a fruit pie followed each other like a row of ducklings, and Jonathan felt that the least he could do, despite paying for the local fare, was to give a concert up to the high standards of the food.

Never far from his mind was the memory of Velvel, so as the other guests finished eating, he decided to start with the composition he had invented for his love. He took out his violin as the innkeeper clapped his hands to end the buzz of conversation around the few dining tables, and he introduced Jonathan.

"Gentlemen, ladies, this young man would like to reward my dear wife for the splendorous repast she prepared for your enjoyment," he said pompously. "And what is his reward, you may ask? No, no, not that! I love my wife!" He guffawed. "Music. Music, music, music! Listen carefully to him. He says he's good. We'll see. Young man..."

Jonathan whispered to himself: "For you, Velvel. For us."

The opening three chords immediately caught the guests' attention. The following brilliant, fast-paced melody held them spellbound. And the final three chords were greeted with as much thunderous applause as can be made by about fifteen guests.

"More, more, more!" they shouted.

Jonathan followed up his opening number with tunes well known to shtetl Jews. Merry melodies played at weddings, nostalgic songs to which the audience sang along, and even some *chazzanut,* liturgical music familiar to those present from shul services, to which the audience swayed back and forth in their seats as if *davening,* praying. His performance was stellar and lasted for well over an hour.

After Jonathan's concert and the copious meal, the travelers, having spent their day on the road, were ready for bed. Local dinner guests said their farewells to the host and to Jonathan who then climbed the stairs to his room at the top of the inn under the roof.

Jonathan was exhausted and fell into a deep sleep. Next morning, as the sun rose, images crept into his awakening consciousness. His parents, standing side by side, tears running unchecked down their cheeks; Velvel smiling up at him; Estherel and Rivkeleh playing with a doll on the floor, looking at him sadly. The face of the doll was that of Naomi. Rabbi Levy, the only one to speak, saying: "You'll be sorry! Very sorry."

Jonathan forced himself into wakefulness and felt the tears on his own cheeks. This was not healthy, he told himself. He must try and put the past where it belonged: behind him. He washed and hastily put on his *tefillin,* his phylacteries, two small leather boxes containing a sacred text held on his head and left arm with leather straps. He recited an abbreviated version of his prayers and then, after removing the ritual objects, he packed them in his suitcase and went down for breakfast.

There was already a smattering of guests in the dining room of the inn. Jonathan took his place at a small table by the window. As ample as his last meal had been, so this, the first of the day, was meager: tea, some dry bread, a tomato, a piece of cheese and a hard-boiled egg. Jonathan saved the cheese and the egg for his lunch, and having finished the slim pickings of his breakfast, he sat gazing out of the window. The coach to Poznan was not due to leave until ten.

"Good morning, young man." A deep male voice roused him from his reverie. Standing at his table was a man whose figure matched his voice: large, self-confident, authoritative but not unkind. He was dressed in a gabardine suit cut to flatter his slightly too ample frame, and he carried a fur-lined cloth coat over his arm.

"Good morning, sir," Jonathan replied automatically.

"May I join you?"

"Please do." The man sat down in the chair facing Jonathan.

"I heard you playing last night. I was very impressed. Are you a professional violinist?"

"Well, yes, but perhaps at the beginning of my career. I am also a student and teacher of Talmud."

"You're traveling, like me. Where are you going?"

"Poznan."

"Ah," said the stranger, "my home town. What plans do you have when you get there?"

"Well, no concrete plans. I'll first go to the largest yeshiva in the city and see the mashgiach. Perhaps I can tutor one or two of the students. Perhaps I can play my violin at some local simchas."

"Young man... What's your name, anyway?"

"Jonathan. Jonathan Brodski." He concentrated on the unfamiliar ring of his new name, making sure that he said it correctly.

"Pleased to meet you, Jonathan. My name is Abraham Pinsky. Where are you from?"

Jonathan was not prepared for this question. In wishing to put his past behind him, he wanted to ensure that nobody could trace his origins. There was no question of telling the truth. Perhaps Abraham Pinsky knew people in Rypin. Perhaps at some point, he would want to investigate Jonathan's past, and nobody in Rypin would have heard of Jonathan Brodski. Similarly, Abraham Pinsky might ask him questions he could not answer about a relatively large Jewish centre. So he had to choose a fairly remote place that Abraham Pinsky was not likely to know.

"I'm from Malbork." Malbork was a small town some distance from Rypin.

"Malbork, Malbork," Abraham Pinsky repeated. "Don't know it." Jonathan gave an inward sigh of relief. "You married? Got a family? I know you're quite young, but I'm just curious."

Once again, Jonathan was taken unawares. He decided on the spur of the moment to say: "Well, I was. That's partly why I'm traveling. Unfortunately, my wife died suddenly in childbirth a year after we were married. Our baby didn't survive, either." Jonathan sent up a silent prayer for Naomi's good health.

"Oh, I'm so sorry. I wish you a long life." The expression was the customary salutation to someone marking the anniversary of a loved one's death.

"I needed to get away, yet as I travel, it seems she's always with me." Jonathan assumed an appropriately sad mien. Some credible excuse had to be invented to avoid his becoming involved in any other nuptial arrangement, at least for the foreseeable future. Grief at his supposed recent loss was as fitting an excuse as any.

"So, Jonathan Brodski, this is your adventure. A new city, a new life. Well, as it happens, I may be able to help you. I may be able to give your career a boost."

Jonathan's interest was piqued. Perhaps luck was on his side. He had never imagined that anyone would propose such a quick solution to his immediate problem – material survival.

"In what way?"

"Jonathan." In view of the offer Abraham Pinsky was about to make, he felt entitled to call Jonathan by his first name alone. "I own a restaurant in Poznan. Not a large restaurant, mind you, but one that gives me and my family a reasonable living. I've even made enough money to send my oldest son to New York. In fact, I'm traveling back to Poznan from Danzig where I bade him farewell. Anyway, back to my restaurant. I'm prepared to offer you a wage you can live on, plus free board and lodging, if you'll play your violin in my restaurant. What do you think of that?"

Jonathan was not sure. He had never worked for anyone else. Would he become dependent on this stranger, not only for his wages but for his living quarters and food?

Abraham Pinsky noticed Jonathan's hesitation. "Come now, you don't have to make an immediate decision. When we reach Poznan, you'll come and see my restaurant, I'll show you where you can stay, and you can even sample the food for free – just one meal, mind – and then you can decide whether or not to accept my offer."

This seemed fair and reasonable to Jonathan so he nodded his assent. When the stagecoach to Poznan drew into the courtyard of the inn at Inowroclaw, Abraham Pinsky approached the coachman and proffered him a healthy tip to secure corner seats opposite each other in the vehicle, one for himself, the other for Jonathan. There were six passengers inside the coach while two others, whose fare was considerably cheaper, sat above, exposed to the elements, next to the coachman.

Abraham Pinsky tried to hold a conversation with Jonathan as the stagecoach creaked over the rough road to Poznan, but the noise of the wheels on the gravel and the general discomfort caused by the poorly-sprung coach eventually reduced them to silence. One or two of the passengers, including Jonathan, managed to doze fitfully despite the discomfort of the conveyance. The others were either lost in their thoughts or gazed apathetically at the landscape rolling past the windows. They all just wanted to arrive.

Toward the end of the afternoon, the coach pulled into the main inn of Poznan. At that time, Poznan and the surrounding Grand Duchy were part of Prussia, which lent a distinctive German character to both the inn and the city beyond it.

However, as Jews lived mainly in shtetls outside the cities and in ghettos within them, the vicissitudes of the political fortunes of the areas they occupied affected them little. They were the butt of occasional anti-Semitic barbs and even physical attacks whatever the prevailing regime, and endeavored to have as little contact with officialdom as possible.

"Come, Jonathan," said Abraham Pinsky, "we'll borrow a trolley and take our luggage to my restaurant. My family and I live in an apartment on the upper floors of the building. If you wish, you can even stay in Benny's room." Benny was his son, now at sea on the way to New York.

Jonathan thanked his prospective employer and then unloaded their bags from the roof of the coach, his being considerably lighter than Mr. Pinsky's, and placed them on a two-wheeled handcart. The men then set off toward the Pinsky restaurant a few blocks away. Jonathan placed his precious violin on top of the bags in its case.

Jonathan was fascinated by the hustle and bustle of this big city. He had never ventured far from Rypin and this was his first time away from his birthplace. The streets echoed with the clatter of vehicles coursing up and down its busy streets. Street vendors touted their wares, sidewalk musicians and clowns solicited coins, beggars roamed through the crowd, richer folk went in and out of small stores. Jonathan did not know where to look first, but he immediately felt comfortable. Here he could be anonymous. More than that, here he could perhaps find a friend or even people like himself.

Within a few minutes, Jonathan and Mr. Pinsky arrived at the restaurant. It was in an old, half-timbered, four-storey building in the ghetto. The restaurant, consisting of about twenty tables and the kitchen, took up the entire ground floor. Everything, from the white tablecloths to the cooking range that Jonathan glimpsed in the kitchen at the back, looked spotlessly clean. At this time of day there were no diners although the chef, his helper and the two waiters were already in place, the chef bustling about in the kitchen preparing the evening meal while the waiters set the tables.

"Come upstairs, my boy, and I'll introduce you to my family and show you my place," said Abraham Pinsky. Jonathan followed him.

"Fraidl," shouted Mr. Pinsky halfway up the stairs, "we have a guest." He pulled his heavy bag up the flight of stairs. Waiting at the top was a buxom lady whose chubby face lit up with a welcoming smile.

"How was your trip, Tatteh?" she asked. "Did Benny get away alright?" Her smile quickly faded as she dabbed a kerchief to her watery eyes. "I miss him already."

"Yes, my dear. I know it was sad to see him go, but he was so excited, and who knows, if things work out well for him, perhaps we'll even join him. Now," he continued "this is Jonathan."

Having entered the spacious apartment, Jonathan inclined his head.

"*Sholom aleichem*" he said, using the traditional greeting of peace.

"*Aleichem sholom.*" Mrs. Pinsky gave the equivalent reply.

"Jonathan is a brilliant violinist who gave us a magnificent concert when we were on the road last night. I'm hoping he'll stay and work for us in the restaurant."

"Wonderful, wonderful," said Mrs. Pinsky. "I can't wait to hear you. Come, you'll join us for dinner, I hope?"

Jonathan was overwhelmed. So much was happening so quickly. The trauma of leaving home was suffused by the fast pace of his new experiences – his concert the previous evening, meeting Abraham Pinsky, the color and cacophony of Poznan and now, this new family. For years, he had followed a steady routine of studying in the yeshiva, playing his music for himself and at family celebrations, peace on shabbes, intellectual challenge during the week, and then came Velvel. And Naomi. And other people trying to control his future. Now, although events were overtaking him, facing him with decisions that had never arisen in the past, he was, nevertheless, forging his own path. The experience stimulated him.

"You're very kind, Mrs. Pinsky. I'm very grateful." Jonathan blushed, confused by this unexpected generosity and the realization of his burgeoning independence.

"Jonathan, can I assume you'll stay with us, at least for tonight?" Mr. Pinsky asked.

"Yes, yes. I would be so happy to do so," said Jonathan. "I'll bring up my things." Jonathan went back downstairs to bring up his bag and his violin. His shtreimel had almost come loose from its attachment outside his suitcase. He then carried his worldly possessions up two more floors to the top of the house where Benny's room was located. It was a small clean room with a bed, a dresser and a washbasin.

He washed his face and returned to the family salon where he was introduced to the two children still living at home, an older sister having already married and moved out.

"This is my daughter, Pessie, and my son, Leibl." The two children, who seemed to be about thirteen and nine, respectively, nodded and smiled.

After their early dinner, Abraham Pinsky asked Jonathan if he would do them the honor of playing the violin for them, in the restaurant. Jonathan agreed and they all went downstairs. How the restaurant had changed! From having been an empty room, the restaurant was now filled with diners and there was almost a party atmosphere. Couples and small families were all talking and laughing among themselves, exchanging news, telling jokes, enjoying the food and the camaraderie.

"Look, Jonathan," said Abraham Pinsky, "I won't introduce you to the people. You just start to play."

Jonathan took out his violin and tuned it. The chatter in the room was so loud that nobody paid any heed to the tuneless sound of the strings. Having accomplished this without attracting attention, Jonathan decided to repeat the niggun he had composed for Velvel. But instead of the three attention-catching chords at the beginning, he would go straight into the first and quietest of the three fast-paced sections of the melody and end each with the three chords.

He closed his eyes. He imagined Velvel standing, smiling before him. He whispered his name. And he played.

At first, the babble in the room continued. When Jonathan reached the first three chords, the people nearest him looked up. As he played the second, slightly louder version, the silence spread like a ripple through the room, and after he had performed the last section with its final three loud chords, the room exploded with applause, the sound contrasting with the audience's previous rapt attention like the crash of a breaking wave.

Jonathan was stunned. He looked blankly at the crowd of cheering diners calling for more. Then a grin spread slowly over his face as he took a bow and waved his violin at his admirers, still applauding wildly. He looked back shyly at the beaming Mr. and Mrs. Pinsky.

"So, Jonathan, go on, give us some more!" shouted Mr. Pinsky, encouraging him.

After playing for another fifteen minutes or so, Jonathan placed his violin under his arm and held up his hand. "Thank you. Thank you everyone. The food is good. You don't want it to get cold. I'll play some more for you later."

The evening was a resounding success. After the last diner had left, Jonathan and Mr. Pinsky sat at one of the tables and agreed on terms of payment. Jonathan would be free during the day to go to the local yeshiva and pursue his Talmudic studies, and in the evenings, except for shabbes, he would play his violin in the restaurant. He would stay in Benny's room with the Pinsky family. That night, when he retired to his room, he told himself, I can succeed and I *will* succeed. Before closing his eyes, he thanked God for both his talent and his good fortune.

Jonathan realized that he might never again find a love like that of Velvel, but in this city his fellow Jews might leave him in peace as a 'widower' and just accept without question the pleasure he could bring them with his music.

"What a relief it must have been for you," I said, "to realize that you could make people happy with your music and also make a living at the same time!"

"Yes. In a way the excitement reduced some of the distress of leaving home. In Poznan, I could be my own person, and people appreciated me for my music. I was no longer seen just as someone who had to perpetuate the family name."

"I had the same feeling when I started a new career as a translator. My clients paid me for my work, not because I was a member of a trade union, an organization formed by workers to protect their interests from exploitation by their employer. As a member of the union, I could not be fired unless I committed a serious offense, so I had no incentive to take any initiative in my work, or even to do anything but the bare minimum. I eventually left my job with the organization of my own accord because I was so bored."

Chapter 2

Jonathan fell into a routine of yeshiva studies during the day and playing music in the evenings. His life was refreshingly absent of any talk of marriage or fear of discovery as a man attracted to other men. Having fabricated the story about being a widower, he could relax for a while and forget about being the object of any mother's marital ambitions for her daughter. Yet the pain of having lost Velvel did not seem to lessen. He thought of him especially at night before falling asleep, wondering where Velvel was and whether he was thinking of him. The image of the glade in which they had made love so often flashed before his eyes. It had never seemed to rain on those Friday afternoons, although sometimes the humidity had made their bodies slick, heightening their passion. Jonathan remembered the texture of Velvel's skin, the sweet smell of his mop of hair and the quick flash of his smile. And then, just before drifting into oblivion, Jonathan felt damp tears on his cheek as the ache of missing his lover invaded his thoughts once more.

Sometimes, in the middle of the night, Jonathan was awakened by the unaccustomed sound of a passing horse and carriage, the clip-clop of hooves and the grating of wheels on the road surface. Disoriented, he wondered why a carriage would be abroad in the streets of Rypin at such an hour, until he realized where he was. How different Poznan was from Rypin! Here, he heard church bells chiming on a Sunday or occasionally tolling for a funeral, something never heard in Rypin. Here, there were stores of every kind frequented by fashionable women and military men of the Prussian army, since Poznan was a major center within East Prussia. The streets buzzed with action, carriages rolling by and pedestrians out shopping or merely meeting acquaintances as they paraded along the boulevards and in the parks on sunny Sundays. Poznan was like another country, another civilization. One could not help but be exposed to life beyond the ghetto. Yet Jonathan, having abandoned his family life in Rypin, was determined not to surrender his Jewish identity too. Losing one pillar of his being was enough of an adaptation. Losing the other, his Judaism, would have brought the whole edifice crashing down.

Thus, on the practical level, shortly after arriving in Poznan and reaching an agreement with Abraham Pinsky, Jonathan had located a yeshiva that measured up to his high academic standards. There had been no problem joining – he had merely asked to see the head of the yeshiva, explained that he had moved to Poznan from Malbork and that he was a widower. The rabbi had immediately welcomed Jonathan to the kollel, the yeshiva study group for married men.

One day, shortly before Rosh Hashonah, Jonathan wound his way through the street crowds on his way to the yeshiva. Suddenly, a short distance in front of him, he noticed a shock of red hair poking out beneath the peaked cap that was almost a uniform for yeshiva students. The man's height was the same as Velvel's, the body shape the same as Velvel's. Jonathan quickened his pace. He caught up with the stranger. It must be him!, he thought. He put his hand on the man's arm.

"Velvel?"

The man turned to face him. It was not Velvel. The twisted nose and frowning forehead could never have been Velvel's. The sallow skin of his cheeks was wrinkled, prematurely aged, reminding Jonathan of fissures spreading, tentacle-like, across a slab of broken ice.

"Oh, oh, I'm sorry. Forgive me, I thought you were someone else."

"It's nothing. Nothing," said the man, moving on.

Jonathan's racing heart plunged to his boots. Not him. How could it not be him? What cruel joke was this? Would it ever be him? Could Jonathan dare to hope that someday, it would be him?

In this downcast mood, Jonathan walked on to the yeshiva class, trying unsuccessfully to put Velvel out of his mind. He was gone. He had disappeared and Jonathan would never be able to find him. He knew he had to accept that. But what chance was there of ever finding someone else like Velvel? Once again, Jonathan was overcome by a feeling of isolation. Yes, the Pinsky family was kind to him. Yes, the diners he entertained appreciated him. But there was no one, not a single soul he could really talk to. He wondered for what purpose God had created him. He could never look forward to having any children and probably no other special person to whom he could devote his love and attention. There was a flaw in his character, an invisible flaw, although everyone had some failing or other. But his flaw had been shared by Velvel who had loved him. So, Jonathan thought, there must be something worth loving in me. His mind drifted back to the journey he had chosen to take away from Rypin and his thoughts at that time. He would be his own mother, his own father, his own son. He was worth loving and if nobody else loved him, he would love himself.

Sometimes, as he prayed in the study hall of the yeshiva with his fellow students, eyes closed and his *tallis,* his prayer shawl, pulled over his head to shut out the world and increase his concentration, Jonathan's thoughts would wander away from the daily liturgy. Each cherished moment spent with Velvel in the forest near Rypin would materialize involuntarily before his eyes. To his embarrassment, the memories occasionally sparked physical arousal. Knowing that his thoughts were sinful, his face became flushed. He would look around to see whether anyone had noticed his discomfort. Fortunately, the other worshippers were so engrossed in their own prayers that they did not notice him. Jonathan wondered whether any of them had distracting thoughts like his, or were they so sincere in their prayers, so caught up in their religious fervor that no extraneous thought ever intruded?

His feeling of aloneness and depression deepened as day followed day leading up to Rosh Hashonah. On the solemn occasion itself, Jonathan accompanied his employer and his son, Leibl, to the shul. It was a time of retrospection on the past year, introspection into his behavior, and anticipation of the coming year. On Rosh Hashonah, God decides who is to be born and who will die in the next year; who will travel and who will remain tranquil; who will become poor and who will become rich – in a word, every individual's fate.

Jonathan looked back over the past year and remembered his family in Rypin. He missed them and felt sad for them, but at the same time he was relieved that what might have occurred, his marriage, had never happened. He was now in control of his own destiny and would succeed or fail on his own merits, in his music as well as in his personal life. He prayed to God to show him the way to become reconciled with the person he was, and to accept whatever lay in store for him. He prayed for the sensitivity to recognize anyone like himself who should cross his path and for the courage to take the risk of getting to know that person. Above all, he prayed for someone in whom he could confide, whom he could get to know and with whom he could share his innermost thoughts.

The *Yomim noro'im,* the Days of Awe following Rosh Hashonah, ended with *Yom Kippur,* the Day of Atonement. Jonathan fasted on that day with the other congregants to atone for their sins, and all the sins that could possibly have been committed by the entire community. Fasting was a mass penitence, covering all eventualities.

In the days following the fast day, he helped Abraham Pinsky and a few of his friends build a large *succah* in the backyard of the restaurant building. It was a temporary structure with a roof of leaves representing the dwellings of the

Israelites during their 40 years of wandering in the desert following the Exodus from Egypt. For the seven days of *Succos,* the festival of Tabernacles, diners would eat outside, in this booth, unless the weather was inclement, to fulfill the mitzvah of the festival. The final day of the holiday season was an added festival, *Simchas Torah,* celebrating the restart of the cycle of weekly readings from the beginning of the Torah, the five books of Moses. Jonathan joined in the dancing in the shul and rejoiced with the men of the community in the gift of Holy Scripture. The women, hidden behind a curtain in their own section, could do no more than try and catch a glimpse of the revelry.

Two weeks after the festivities, the weather turned cold, and in the next week, the first snow fell. Jonathan's spirits fell with it. Once again, he realized that any social contact he made would have to come through the kollel of which he, as a 'widower', was now a member.

Chapter 3

During his first few weeks in Poznan Jonathan studied at his new yeshiva, he had four nondescript chevrusas. He felt no spark of friendship for any of them. They were all family men who showed no interest in Jonathan as an individual. They attended the yeshiva to study. That was all. Jonathan's fifth chevrusa was different.

Herschel Kaufman was also a family man with a wife and six children. He had been blessed with a naturally curious mind and seemed to want to know every detail about everything and everyone. He was in his forties, slightly balding, with a narrow face and a short beard. But the feature that shone from his face was a beautiful set of white teeth, often revealed in his frequent smile. On his first day as Jonathan's chevrusa he started chatting during a tea break.

"So, Jonathan, where are you from?"

Jonathan had to think twice. "I'm from Malbork. Yes, I'm from Malbork," said Jonathan, relieved at having remembered the name.

"Malbork? Don't know it."

"It's a small shtetl in the north. Not big."

"And your wife? Your family?"

"Unfortunately, I lost my dear wife soon after we were married." That part of his story Jonathan had no difficulty in remembering.

"I'm sorry, I'm sorry. Perhaps I ask too many questions."

"Not at all. It's good to meet someone with a little interest in others."

Over the winter, their friendship blossomed. Jonathan discovered that Herschel Kaufman had even read secular books of both a literary and scientific nature. He was a mine of information on many subjects previously unknown to Jonathan. On Friday afternoons, when the yeshiva closed for shabbes, they would take short walks, or Jonathan would invite Herschel to the Pinsky restaurant for a glass of tea, where they would sit at one of the empty tables and talk endlessly. Of special fascination to the two friends was the burgeoning Reform movement in Judaism. Originating in Germany after the Napoleonic age, this new stream of Judaism was revolutionary, questioning many of the basic tenets of Judaism and adapting them to the customs of the dominant Christian society. While intrigued by this philosophy, both Jonathan and Herschel rejected it as too radical. Even circumcision, the Jewish covenant with God, was no longer practiced by members of the new movement, *kashrut,* the eating of kosher food, was abandoned, and Saturday as the Sabbath day was replaced by Sunday.

Toward the spring, shortly before Passover, their friendship took on a more personal note. It was early on a Friday afternoon as they sat alone in the Pinsky restaurant that Herschel asked:

"Have you never thought of marrying again, Jonathan?"

"Herschel, it's something I don't like to discuss. I was very close with my wife, and I still miss her a lot."

"But it's only natural. A man needs a woman."

Jonathan looked down at his glass. Should he trust this man? Herschel had always been open with him, revealing things about his own personal life and his family relationships not usually discussed between men. Herschel had been born into an unhappy family, his mother in constant conflict with his father. Nevertheless, there had been five siblings. Eventually, his father had abandoned the family and run off with another woman. His mother, unable to support her children, had farmed them out to relatives, and Herschel had been brought up by an uncle and aunt. Other confidences followed about his own family, but Herschel had never been indiscreet. Without any doubt he loved his wife and children. Perhaps, Jonathan thought, I should delve a little deeper into this relationship and take it further. He dared to make an unconventional statement.

"Not all men need a woman," he said flatly.

It was Herschel's turn to look down at his tea. "I'm not sure I understand you. Are you saying that you don't need a woman?" The question was asked without any ill will or hint of accusation. It was a frank inquiry from a friend.

"Yes," Jonathan almost whispered. An uncomfortable moment of silence passed between them. "Herschel, I don't know whether you can understand but I want you to know. You're my friend and I want to keep you as my friend. Please try to understand." Jonathan had never considered Herschel as anything but a friend. Any other thought or ambition had never occurred to him.

"Jonathan, I do want to understand. But I need some explanation. What are you telling me?"

"Can I trust you, Herschel? Can you keep a secret? Are you strong enough to remain my friend no matter what I tell you?"

"Trust me, Jonathan. You *can* trust me."

Jonathan leaned back in his chair. Perhaps at last the sense of isolation he had experienced over these past few months in Poznan was over.

"Herschel, I have lied to you. To everyone. But it was for my own protection. I have never been married. Women hold no attraction for me. No physical attraction."

"You mean you don't feel any attraction at all? What can you be attracted to besides women?"

"There are other people besides women, Herschel."

"The only other people are men." Herschel's voice was unsure as the possibility dawned on him. He did not want to offend or frighten his friend. "Jonathan, do you mean men? You're attracted to men?"

"Not any man, but yes. I find an attractive man... attractive," said Jonathan awkwardly.

Herschel sat silently for a few moments. "Jonathan, we both know that this is considered an abomination. Is there no way you can choose otherwise?"

"Herschel, believe me, if there were any way I could choose I would do so. But I can no more choose than you can. I have never felt any other way. I enjoy the company of the few women I have known, but I have no desire for them. It's something quite different in the case of men, or should I say a man I find attractive."

"So how have you managed? Does anyone else know of your situation?"

"I have managed with great difficulty. It hasn't been easy. And a few people do know about me, which is the reason I am here." Jonathan was not ready to divulge all his reasons for leaving Rypin and his family to Herschel until he was assured of Herschel's positive reaction to his confession.

Herschel considered what Jonathan had said. How would he himself have reacted in Jonathan's place? Could he have changed? He imagined the reverse circumstances. Could he force himself to make love with a man? Never! But what if his natural instinct had been to desire a man instead of a woman? Although he had no notion of how he would physically consummate a relationship with a man, he did have some idea of how a man could be emotionally attracted and attached to another man. After all, he felt great affection for Jonathan himself, although the idea of anything more than that had never occurred to him. But if he could feel affection for Jonathan, surely he should feel sympathy for him. Even empathy. Jonathan had said he would change if he could. His desire to conform was there; his ability to do so was not. Herschel understood.

"Jonathan," he said, "I'm so sorry." He put his hand on Jonathan's on the tabletop and squeezed it. "I'll do anything I can to help you. I do realize how lonely it must have been for you and how you must have suffered... Yes, we must talk more about this. I promise it will go no further. Don't worry. We'll talk again about this."

He rose from the table. "I must go. Your secret will be completely safe with me, Jonathan. Shabbes is here. Eat well, pray well and relax. Now I have to bathe and go to the *mikve*, the ritual bath. I wish you a *gut shabbes*, and I'll see you on Sunday." He left.

Jonathan remained at the table, cradling his glass in his hands. Had he done the right thing? He had no choice. The loneliness was destroying his peace of mind. Now, at least, he could talk about it, talk about his family, talk about Velvel and even, perhaps, about Naomi. Jonathan's shell had been broken and a new chapter could begin.

"You were so lucky, Jonathan, to have found Herschel," I said.

"Yes I was. It was almost a love affair without any physical element."

"I, on the other hand, have never succeeded in having a meaningful friendship with a man unlike myself, a man who desired women. Perhaps I seemed threatening to other men. I wonder whether their attraction for the opposite sex somehow excludes a deep relationship with another man."

"It didn't in my case," asserted Jonathan.

Chapter 4

Jonathan spent the Sabbath in a state of euphoria. Although he had not found a replacement for Velvel, which was perhaps too much to expect, he had found a personal point of human contact. Herschel was already a friend, one whom he knew well and whom he felt he could trust. Herschel had shared some personal details with Jonathan and now Jonathan felt he could reciprocate that trust.

As Jonathan mulled over this new, refreshing turn in his life, he realized how Herschel could, indeed, help him. There had been no contact with his family since he had left Rypin, nor did he wish to reveal his new identity to them. Any letters they sent to him would not reach him if addressed to his former name, but Herschel could help overcome this problem. Following their study session on Sunday, Jonathan asked Herschel to remain behind after the evening prayer.

"Herschel, I've been thinking… There is a way you can help me. I have not been in touch with my family since I left home shortly before Rosh Hashonahh. I would like to write to them and hear from them. But when I left, I changed my name. I wanted to become a different person, my own person. So I want to ask you a favor."

"Of course. Anything …"

"In the letter I plan to send to my parents, I would like to give your name for them to write to. I would not give them your address because I don't want them to try and trace me through you. I could ask the people at the inn to accept a letter addressed to you, and they could send their reply to me there. Would you allow me to do that?"

"Of course, my dear friend. The people at the inn will let me know when I receive a letter, and I can just give it to you."

"Herschel, you don't know how grateful I am." He took Herschel's hand in his and shook it warmly. "If I can ever return the favor..."

Jonathan raced back to the restaurant and, after giving his usual performance to Abraham Pinsky's dinner guests, he climbed the stairs to his room, physically tired but mentally alert, to pen his first letter from Poznan to his family. He briefly closed his eyes, imagining them receiving and opening his letter, relieved at reading his news. He wrote:

> *My dear Mommeh, my dear Tatteh:*
>
> *I am here, in Poznan, where I came after leaving you and Rypin. I often think about you and hope you are well and have come to accept my reason for leaving. It was a decision I had to make for everyone's good, and my only regret was having to hurt you all in the process.*
>
> *I am staying with a wonderful family. I met the father on my way here. I have also found work, playing the violin in a restaurant.*

Jonathan did not want to tell them that the family he was staying with also owned the restaurant. That would make him more easily traceable.

> *By day, I study at a yeshiva, and I play in the restaurant in the evening. I am as happy as possible but, of course, I miss you all very much. I would like to hear from you, to find out how you are and to receive news of Rivkeleh and Estherel. Please give them both my love.*

I am asking you to send your reply to a friend. Please indulge me. I now have a new life and even a new name.

Again, I ask for your forgiveness for the pain I have caused you. Please write to me.

Your loving son,
Yankl

Jonathan signed his former name, one that had now become so unfamiliar to him. He addressed the envelope and kissed it, making sure to add Herschel's name and that of the inn where his parents' reply could be picked up. The next day he took it to the inn to pay for the delivery by coach.

Jonathan's outlook on life was transformed by his friendship with Herschel. He could now communicate with someone, relieved to be able to talk about his reason for leaving Rypin, about the inevitability of his decision and about the pain he was sure he had caused in so doing. He also expressed to Herschel his own grief at having caused that pain and for having relinquished his former life in the process. Herschel understood how impossible it had been for Jonathan to withstand the strong pressure to get married, and that escape was the only way out. But for the present, Jonathan decided not to mention his love affair with Velvel or the story of their discovery and confrontation with Rabbi Levy.

Meanwhile, Jonathan's letter was delivered to the Bradawka family. Leah took it from a boy sent from the inn. She looked at the envelope and saw Yankl's name on it. The agonizing pain she had suffered when he left was still as strong as ever for her. It was even too great for her to open the letter. She was incapable of facing the possibility of more suffering. For the time being, she placed the envelope unopened in the bottom of a drawer containing her underwear. Nobody would find it there. When she felt calmer, she would read it.

She and her husband, Mendl, had emerged from their loss to the point of concealing their grief from their two daughters. For their sake they put on a stoic face at the disappearance of their only son. It had not been easy. For six days they had sat shiva for Yankl, with visitors coming to console them, starting with ma'ariv held in the house. Before they arrived, Mendl would carry his two daughters next door to Mrs. Chaskel's house, where they snuggled down on her couch at their bedtime. The novelty of the situation provided a welcome distraction to the girls' obvious distress at the absence of their beloved brother. It also served to keep them away from any gossip concerning Yankl's departure.

The worst moment of the shiva period for Mendl and Leah Bradawka had been when Mr. and Mrs. Schneider came to pay their respects.

Hannah Schneider had entered the room ahead of her husband, Otto. She had been much affected by her daughter Naomi's sense of loss. Naomi had taken her fiancé's flight hard. She felt rejected and, in spite of Yankl's note to her, she believed somehow that she was to blame for the failure of the match. Naomi had discussed Yankl's "incurable disease" with her parents. Nothing in his demeanor had given a clue as to what it might be, whether physical or mental. Yet, curious as they were as to the nature of Yankl's disease, they realized that it would be indelicate to question his parents about it.

Hannah had tried to get her daughter to come to terms with the situation, but realized that Naomi, too, had to pass through a grieving process. Nevertheless, the prospect of intensifying Naomi's sorrow by having her visit the Bradawkas was never even contemplated. Her parents went alone.

On entering the Bradawka house, Hannah went first to the kitchen to leave a roast chicken she had cooked for the bereaved family. She placed it on the counter with other gifts of food brought by wives in the community so that the family would not have to bother with buying and preparing food. In times of personal crisis, the community never failed to come together in support of those suffering.

Hannah then turned to the living room. She hesitated at the threshold. It was the custom to let mourners speak first to those who came to comfort them, leaving the bereaved the choice of whether to speak and reach out, or to remain barricaded within the fortress of their sorrow. There were other visitors in the room as Hannah entered but Leah Bradawka noticed Hannah immediately. Silent tears spilled from her eyes. Hannah crossed the room, knelt before Leah and took her in her arms, both women now crying openly. Otto followed his wife and held out both hands to Mendl who held onto them like a lifeline. For a few moments, the room fell silent, all eyes focused on the two distraught couples.

"We are so sorry," whispered Hannah.

"And we are so grateful that you have come to share this sad time with us," replied Leah, withdrawing from Hannah's embrace so as to put the other visitors at ease. Conversation in the room resumed.

"We shall never forget you and Naomi," said Mendl to Otto, "and we can never forgive Yankl for what he has done to you, and to us."

Otto Schneider pulled up two chairs, one for himself and one for his wife, so as to be able to sit and talk more comfortably with the Bradawkas, seated on their low shiva chairs.

"You know, Leah," said Hannah, "Yankl left a note for Naomi. Naomi said she would not mind if I showed it to you. Do you want to see it?"

Leah read the note. Few of the words registered with her except for Yankl's confession of suffering from an incurable disease and his request to Naomi not to blame his parents for creating this awful situation. Leah had never believed that her son was intrinsically evil, and his note to Naomi confirmed this belief. As for his incurable disease, Leah was grateful that Yankl had not revealed the true details of his condition.

"Hannah, thank you. I cannot absorb all that has happened yet. I cannot take in what Yankl has written in this note. Perhaps when we are over the worst, when we manage to accept this, later, I'll be able to read it again. I can only apologize for upsetting you and Otto so much, and of course, Naomi. Such a sweet girl..."

"Leah, there's no need to apologize. Naomi will get over it, I'm sure. You are the ones who will eventually have to live with this, and Otto and I wish you strength. Your little girls will give you that strength. They will grow and marry and make you happy again."

"Hannah, perhaps one day I will be able to see things that way. Meanwhile, we have lost our only son."

There was nothing more Hannah could think of to say. She took Leah's hands in hers and kissed them. The action expressed more than any words she could have thought of.

Chapter 5

Somehow, the Bradawka family got through the days of shiva. Despite the visits of caring friends and sympathetic acquaintances, the pain of their loss invaded their thoughts at night, alone in the dark of their beds. Their tears flowed unbidden as they remembered their son's small acts of kindness and his music, and each night their anguish seemed to deepen rather than fade.

After the shiva period, some sort of routine began to re-establish itself, Leah again preparing food for her reduced family and Mendl returning to his butcher shop. Yankl's chair stood empty at mealtimes, a constant reminder of his absence, until a few days later when Mendl removed it from the table and placed it against a wall.

Shortly thereafter, a boy came to Mendl's shop with a request from Rabbi Levy to go and see him. Mendl closed his little store early and walked over to the shul, slightly apprehensive. What could the rabbi want now?

"Come in Mendl. Please, sit down," the rabbi said from behind the desk in his study. "There's one last thing about Yankl we have to discuss." Mendl sat down.

"Mendl, I know what a difficult time this has been for you, your dear wife and daughters. Yankl was a perfectly normal boy who yielded to an evil temptation, an abomination, and as a result, he defied both you and me. He rejected our way of life and we must ensure that he has no power to poison the life of anyone else in any community he finds himself."

Mendl said nothing. The constant cloud he felt hovering over his head grew even darker.

"I must pronounce a *cherem,* a proclamation of excommunication, against him."

Mendl sucked in his breath and a sob escaped his lips. He lifted his hands to cover his face, trying vainly to shut out the reality of the moment. He knew the word *cherem,* but he did not know all that it involved.

"Rabbi, what will that mean for Yankl?"

"Mendl, it will not be easy. I have the document here. I'll read some of it to you." The rabbi took a parchment from a drawer in his desk and read from it.

> *After the judgment of the angels and with that of the saints, we excommunicate, expel and curse and damn Yankl Bradawka with the consent of God. The Lord will not pardon him, the anger and wrath of the Lord will rage against this man…*

Mendl slumped in his seat. The rabbi droned on:

> *We order that nobody should communicate with him orally or in writing, or show him any favor, or stay with him under the same roof, or come within four paces of him, or read anything composed or written by him.*

Mendl took a few moments to calm himself. The silence became oppressive. Finally, he spoke.

"Rabbi, this is so difficult for us," he said hoarsely. "Please, before you issue this decree, let me have a little time to think about it. It has been hard enough losing him, having to mourn him, and now this. Can you wait a few days? Please?" he begged.

"Until next week, then. I will do this for you because of your position in the community. But I tell you, this is the right thing to do. And that will be the end of it."

Mendl rose to leave. He could not bring himself to even bid the rabbi a good evening. He shuffled out of the study like a ghost in a nightmare. This was an experience he had already lived when the rabbi told him that he and Leah had to sit shiva for their son. Now the rabbi wished to cut his son off not only from his family but from his people, everywhere. Well, thought Mendl, if he's dead to us, why not to his people, too?

"You're late," said Leah as Mendl stumbled through the door. "It's not like you."

"I had to see the rabbi."

"The rabbi? What did he want?" Leah already felt a certain animosity toward the rabbi. Could he not have just let Yankl live in peace? Why had he tried to force him into a marriage?

"Sit down, Mommeh," said Mendl wearily. "Girls, go and play in your room upstairs. We'll eat in a few minutes."

"Now what?" Leah said as the girls left. She expected the worst from the rabbi, that man of religion who, she felt, had been at the root of all their unhappiness.

"Rabbi Levy wants to take a drastic step that will bring this terrible situation to a final conclusion." Leah waited and braced herself.

"What? What is it?"

"He wants to pronounce a cherem against Yankl."

Anger engulfed Leah like a sheet of fire. Had they not done enough? Now the rabbi wanted to banish her son from his people everywhere. Did she and Mendl have to broadcast their shame and share their loss with the entire Jewish world? She turned away from her husband to hide her fury. Forcing herself to speak calmly, she said, "And you, Tatteh, what do you think of it?"

"Oy, Leah, I can't think anymore. He's given me a few days to accept his decision. What can I say?" Mendl rocked backward and forward in his chair, his pain challenging his belief in God.

A strange tranquility flowed over Leah. She knew what she had to do.

"Perhaps Rabbi Levy will think better of it. Giving you a few days to accept his decision will give him a few days to reconsider it. Come, Tatteh, let's eat. You'll feel better. You'll see things more clearly. Call the girls down." Nothing more was said about the matter that evening. Leah Bradawka, however, knew exactly what she had to do.

The next morning, as soon as Mendl left for work, Leah went next door and asked Mrs. Chaskel if she would be kind enough to take the girls while she ran an errand.

"I won't be long, Mrs. Chaskel. A couple of hours at the most."

"Take your time, my dear. Your girls are no trouble at all."

Leah put on her only hat, the one she wore when she went to shul for the High Holy Days. She left the house and let her feet take her toward the study hall. A bitter wind matched the icy anger in her heart, which she curbed with difficulty. She gathered her thin coat around her. This man would not murder her son's very soul.

Unlike her previous visit to the study hall, she did not ask a stranger to act as her messenger. She walked boldly through the double doors of the building and directly into the study hall. Women never entered this inner sanctum of male exclusivity and as Leah saw the young men studying in couples, their individual sing-song combining into a steady hum, she was at first disconcerted. But the thought of her son dying physically, psychologically and spiritually gave her strength. As one, two, then three and more of the youths noticed her, a fog bank of silence rolled over the room. All eyes in the hushed room turned to her.

At the front of the hall, Rabbi Levy had been discussing the Torah portion of the week with a group of six of the younger boys. As quiet descended on his students, he looked up and noticed Leah Bradawka. It took no more than a moment for him to realize why she had entered the study hall in such an unorthodox fashion. Mendl Bradawka had evidently told his wife about the cherem and she was here to reverse his rabbinical decision. He determined she would not succeed. Over the heads of the young students, the rabbi and the mother stared each other down, neither willing to lower their gaze. Rabbi Levy refused to honor Leah Bradawka's presence by addressing her directly. Neither, he admitted to himself, was he prepared to risk a scene with her in front of his students. He would send an emissary and see her privately in his study. He therefore asked one of the boys in his small group to go and accompany Mrs. Bradawka to his study. The sound of the boy's footsteps seemed amplified as he passed among the study hall desks.

"Rabbi Levy will see you in a few minutes in his study. Please follow me."

"Thank the rabbi for sparing me a little of his valuable time," Leah said to the boy, spicing her politeness with a touch of sarcasm. As Leah followed the boy across the hall, a few nervous coughs from the other students punctuated their progress.

"Please have a seat," the boy said as he left Leah alone in the rabbi's study.

Leah sat in the guest chair in front of the rabbi's large desk. She looked around at the walls of bookshelves overflowing with sacred works. They spilled out onto the floor in stacks among other papers. The slightly musty smell of the holy books sparked her memory of their last interview in this same room, when she and Mendl had heard Rabbi Levy's painful revelation of Yankl's relationship. And, she thought as she returned to the present, where is the humanity, where is the compassion in all these books? A few moments later, Rabbi Levy strode in. He left the study door open – it would have been improper for the rabbi to be in the presence of a woman behind a closed door.

Leah rose from her chair out of respect.

"You may sit, Mrs. Bradawka," the rabbi said formally. "So what was so important that you had to barge into our study hall to see me? Could you not have sent someone in to tell me you were here?" Leah sat down. She ignored the question, and looked directly at the rabbi seated in the large chair behind his desk, an immodest act for a married woman. After a few moments she said:

"How do you feel, Rabbi Levy?" It was an impertinent, personal question.

"What do you mean, how do I feel? How should I feel?"

"Well, rabbi, since you ask me, I'll tell you. You should feel ashamed."

The rabbi winced. He fidgeted in his chair. He had never experienced such a confrontation before, and this from a woman. He felt like a spider on a kitchen wall, about to be smashed into oblivion.

"Why should I feel ashamed?" he ventured.

"For trying to murder my son, your student, my only son."

"Murder?" Rabbi Levy stood as color rose to his cheeks. "How dare you accuse me of murder!" he bellowed. "Who do you think you are? How dare you challenge my authority?" The sound of the rabbi's raised voice traveled down the corridor and into the study hall, where the boys' whispers were again hushed into silence.

It was Leah's turn to rise. Fire burned in her eyes. "I am a mother," she said in a quiet voice, "a Jewish mother of a Jewish son. He may be dead to you. You made us demonstrate that he is dead to this community. But he is not dead, rabbi. For me he will never be dead. And I will not let you murder him. Yes, murder him, Rabbi Levy. My son is a good Jew, a religious Jew, and a good person. If you cast him out of every Jewish community, he will not survive. Your solution of marriage for him did not work. We lost him. You lost him. You made us sit shiva for our only son." Leah spoke through her tears of anger and despair. "And now you want to remove him from the Jewish world? How can a religious Jew survive outside of his community? Is he some sort of miracle like a fish that breathes out of water? Have you no humanity? Imagine if it were your son. Your son instead of ours. You have already put us through enough." Leah sank back onto her chair, exhausted, allowing her silent tears to run freely down her cheeks but still looking directly at the rabbi. "It is enough," she echoed.

Rabbi Levy was stunned. He, too, sat down again, taken aback by her outburst. He said nothing, closing his eyes to try and blot out the distressing scene. Leah's anguished voice pierced the silence.

"Please, Rabbi, if you have any mercy in your soul, do not do this thing. Yankl has left us. He is alone in the world. Do not turn that world against him."

"But, Leah, he has sinned," the rabbi said, more sympathetically. "His sin is called an abomination."

"Rabbi, who among us has not sinned? Yankl is dead to us, but his life continues, somewhere. We shall never know where. Please, let him live in peace."

The rabbi remained silent. He felt obliged to consider Leah Bradawka's plea for her son. But how could he rationalize it? How could he lose face before a mere woman? On the other hand, Mendl and Leah Bradawka were respected members of his community. He found their distress painful and sent up a silent prayer seeking a resolution to this difficult situation. His fear was that Yankl, wherever he ended up in the Jewish world, would corrupt other young men and entice them into his evil ways. Yet, when he looked objectively at what had transpired, Velvel had not been an unwilling or an unwitting partner in Yankl's sin. It was not as if Yankl had entrapped Velvel. How likely was Yankl to lead others astray, and what was that remote possibility compared to the real pain of his distraught parents, a couple for whom the rabbi felt real affection? The rabbi decided to opt for time in order to find a way out of his dilemma.

"Leah, Mendl asked me for a few days to accept my decision. I gave him those few days. I want to help you. I do not enjoy seeing people dear to me, like Mendl and you, suffer. Your words have touched me. So I ask you, in turn, please give me a few days to see how we can avoid this situation. Then I will speak to Mendl and tell him my decision."

Leah finally took her eyes off the rabbi. She bowed her head. Should she apologize for her intrusion? No, she told herself. I would do it again with no hesitation. Her Yankl would survive.

"Thank you, Rabbi Levy," she said simply, rising to leave the room.

"I wish you and Mendl strength, Leah."

At the door, Leah turned to face him. "Rabbi Levy, my husband does not know that I came to see you, and I would be most grateful if you would not tell him." The rabbi nodded to her as she left the study, closing the door behind her. He leaned back in his chair, pondering the situation. Sometimes, he said to himself, the best action is no action. He resolved not to speak to Mendl about the cherem, nor to do anything further about it.

One evening about two weeks later, Mendl said to Leah: "Strange… Rabbi Levy has never mentioned the cherem to me again." Mendl had heard of his wife's unusual visit to see Rabbi Levy in the study hall, but had resisted asking her about it, suspecting her motive. "I wonder whether that…" he wanted to use the right words "that curious visit of yours to the study hall had anything to do with it."

"Perhaps God has shown him the light" said his wife, "and, with Yankl gone. . ." She shrugged, leaving the sentence unfinished, and Mendl asked no further questions.

Chapter 6

Golda Gambiner missed Velvel to the point of mourning for her son. She lost her appetite for food and often cried herself to sleep, unheard by her gently snoring husband. Nothing could console her. Occasionally, the family would receive a letter from Velvel who tried to be positive about his new yeshiva. But with a mother's instinct, Golda discerned the sadness hidden behind the words. She was not sure whether it was his family or his illicit lover that Velvel missed; not that it mattered. What mattered was that he was unhappy, and therefore she, his mother, was unhappy.

For some reason – perhaps Velvel's naïve vulnerability – he was her favorite, although she never gave him preferential treatment over his two brothers. She recalled the story of Joseph and his brothers in Genesis, the first book of the Torah, illustrating how favoritism could lead to jealousy among siblings. But the scar Velvel's banishment to Vilna left in her life never seemed to heal. Worse still, there was nobody to whom she could express her pain at losing him. How could she question Rabbi Levy's decree exiling her son? Her anguish, borne in silence, festered within her.

The Gambiners had invited Golda's sister, Bayla, and her husband, Lazer Goldstein to spend the eight days of *Succos*, the festival of Tabernacles, with them. The Goldsteins lived in a small town a day's journey from Rypin, and since they had not been blessed with children, they preferred to be with family rather than remain alone. The two sisters enjoyed a close relationship, especially since there were no other female relatives with whom they could exchange confidences.

On arriving at the Gambiner home, Golda immediately told her sister and brother-in-law the supposedly good news about Velvel.

"He's been awarded a place at a yeshiva in... Warsaw," said Golda, maintaining the fiction about her son's actual whereabouts. The Goldsteins congratulated the Gambiners on the promotion of their son, wishing them mazel tov, and for a few days nothing more was said.

On the shabbes in the middle of the festival, the two women, not obliged by Jewish custom to attend shul services, stayed home. All the food for the holy day had been prepared the day before as usual, and it was their private time to enjoy together. They sat in the small family room, chatting inconsequentially. Golda saw her opportunity.

"Bayla, I must tell you something, to be kept strictly between ourselves. It's been preying on my mind for weeks, and there's nobody else I can talk to about this."

"It's Sholom, isn't it?" Bayla said, jumping to conclusions about her sister's marriage.

"No, it's not about Sholom. It's about Velvel."

"I thought you said he was doing so well in Warsaw."

"Probably he is doing well there. But I didn't tell you the whole truth about why he was sent there." She paused, twisting a kerchief in her hands. Involuntarily, the tears began to trickle down her cheeks as she put her arms around her body and rocked backward and forward, holding herself as if she were her own child.

Bayla was taken aback by this unexpected show of emotion. Uncertain as to how to react, she slid her chair close to that of her sister and put her arm around her shoulders.

"Golda, what has happened to make you so unhappy?" she said softly. "What has Velvel done?"

"Velvel was sent away because he did something wrong here," Golda blurted out.

"Golda, tell me what happened. How bad could it have been?"

With an effort, Golda composed herself. Her sister shifted her chair to face her. "Velvel became… He became involved with someone…"

Bayla coaxed her. "Involved with someone? Someone… unsuitable? What was her name?"

"It wasn't a woman. Bayla. He was seen with another man." She pronounced the words with a mixture of resignation and relief.

"Another man? So what could be wrong with that?"

"Bayla, Bayla, not just with another man. They were…" Her voice faded out.

"Please, Golda, explain to me what happened."

Golda lifted her head. "They were kissing. Imagine, two men kissing! He thought it was love. And he's so hurt, Bayla. I'm so hurt. We're all so hurt," she said resentfully.

"Kissing? Two men? How is that possible? Who was the other man? And what's become of him?"

"I don't know Bayla. The rabbi wouldn't tell us."

"But Golda, you must have some idea. Who was he spending time with? Was he seeing someone outside the yeshiva, even outside the shtetl?"

Until that moment, Golda Gambiner and her husband had had no inkling of who Velvel's partner could have been. Since his banishment about six weeks before, grief had clouded any speculation on that subject. But like a battering ram smashing through a fortified door, the truth crashed into Golda's mind. The yeshiva. Velvel's chevrusa who had left Rypin days before his marriage. He had refused to marry and his parents had sat shiva for him. Velvel's accomplice in sin had been his chevrusa, Yankl Bradawka.

Golda covered her eyes with her hand.

"Bayla, I know. I know who it was. I've just realized." She explained to her sister who her son's chevrusa had been and what had happened to him and his parents. And so the story was told. Golda let her grief pour out, spilling all her suppressed emotions to her sister's sympathetic ear. Bayla could do no more than try to comfort her.

"Golda, Velvel's away now. Time will heal his sickness, believe me. This was just a passing phase. He's in different surroundings – a new yeshiva, a new life. You'll see, they'll find him a nice girl."

"Well, I'm not sure whether it's a girl he wants, but I can only hope you're right. Perhaps with our prayers and God's help, he will grow out of it. Anyway, Bayla, thank you for listening to me. At least, by having someone to talk to, I feel a little better about it now."

That night, burdened by the weight of her conversation with her sister, Bayla told her husband, Lazer, about it. Not the most discreet of men, at the morning service in shul he was curious to find out further details and made some unsubtle inquiries of a fellow worshipper about the relationship between Velvel and his chevrusa. Through his careless questioning, he unwittingly revealed the motive for his curiosity and, little by little, the gossip spread. Folk in the shtetl then made the link between Velvel Gambiner's sudden departure and the disappearance of Yankl Bradawka, his chevrusa, a few weeks later.

It took about six weeks before the *rebbitzin*, the rabbi's wife, got wind of the story and repeated it to her husband. Rabbi Levy was furious. The sentence he had imposed on Velvel for his sin was his expulsion from the community, but in a way, Yankl had expelled the community from his life. He had, so to speak, escaped the wrath of the shtetl and avoided doing penance. That was something the rabbi could not accept. After all, by doing nothing, people might assume that he tolerated the situation.

So in spite of Leah Bradawka's plea to him, the day after learning that the full story had become public knowledge, Rabbi Levy took the radical step of excommunicating Yankl Bradawka, pronouncing the dreaded cherem upon his head.

He read the text to the students in the yeshiva and a poster to that effect was displayed on the doors of the study hall. Yankl Bradawka was to be totally excluded from the Jewish community everywhere. Nobody was to offer him any support, moral or material, or to have any contact with him. And the decree was then circulated to all the rabbis and major yeshivas in Poland, Lithuania, the Ukraine and Russia.

That next November morning the weather was bitter, the wind biting. Mendl Bradawka learned of his son's cherem as he went to the morning service in the shul and saw the poster. Mendl read the notice. His son, Yankl Bradawka, was cursed. He was to be ostracized by every Jew and was to be refused any shelter, succor and even the merest communication.

Mendl drew his thin winter coat more closely around his shoulders and retreated within himself. Not one of the other men greeted him in the shul, and all avoided his gaze. It did not matter to him. All Mendl could contemplate was the suffering this would cause his son, and the shame to the name of Bradawka.

Leah Bradawka was crushed when she heard of the rabbi's action. All her fears for her son would be realized. It was as though she went through another period of mourning. She also felt betrayed by the rabbi. Despite her desperate appeal, he had made the decision to destroy her son.

One afternoon, a day or two after hearing about the cherem, alone in the bedroom, resting and agonizing over her son's fate, she remembered Yankl's letters – by then, she had received several. She ached to know where he was creating his new life. She thought about the cherem – no contact with the excommunicated person. She thought about her interview with the rabbi a few months before. Then she thought about her son again. She rose from the bed and opened the drawer containing Yankl's letters, neatly arranged in order. She wiped away her tears and read the first one. Then she reread it. Her eyes seized upon one of Yankl's phrases like a cat pouncing on a feather. Yankl had written: I now have a new life and even a new name.

A new name. Her Yankl was no longer Yankl. Leah smiled. Then she started to laugh. Yankl Bradawka had been excommunicated. They had excommunicated a man who no longer existed. They had wanted to wipe him out, but he had done the job for them. Her son had been reborn under another name and the cherem would be totally ineffective. Her darling son Yankl would live. Leah could not stop laughing.

At the evening meal, Mendl Bradawka could not understand his wife's high spirits. She even joked with the girls when playing with them after their dinner. Mendl asked no questions. He merely thanked God for having restored Leah at least to a semblance of her former self.

Chapter 7

The months passed. Jonathan received no reply from his parents. Herschel even went to the inn to make sure that no letter had been received for him and perhaps mislaid. At the approach of every Jewish holy day, Jonathan would write again to his parents. And every time Leah received the letter – it was always delivered during the day, when Mendl was at work – she would read it eagerly, then place it with the others at the bottom of the drawer containing her underclothes.

Jonathan became accustomed to his parents' silence. His close companionship with Herschel replaced in a way the love he had received in the past from his parents. Jonathan pondered the nature of that love. His parents' love for him had, indeed, been conditional. If he had fitted their mold and been the person they wished him to be, he would have retained their affections. However, their love for him had given way under the pressure of convention. It had disintegrated at what they thought the community expected of him, and of them. It was beyond their conception to try and understand that their son could love another man, not just mentally but physically. Rabbi Levy had revealed to them the nature of his relationship with Velvel. For his parents, it was no more than unnatural lust. For them, love could never enter the equation.

Thank God for Herschel, thought Jonathan as he came to this realization. Unconditional love. That was what he had prayed for on Rosh Hashonahh, and that was what God had granted him. It was this mental and emotional communion that enabled him to suppress the physical urges that still invaded his fantasies and plagued his body.

For Herschel, his friendship with Jonathan was a release and a relief from the daily domestic situation in which he found himself. Naturally, he loved his wife, Gittel, and their six young children. He still found his wife physically attractive despite the hard life she led. Indeed, although she loved her career, she was well aware that, as the family's primary breadwinner, she was fulfilling a great mitzvah by enabling her husband to pursue his holy mission of a life devoted to study. Not only did she have six young children to worry about, but she had to work to supplement the small charitable stipend Herschel received for studying at the yeshiva. She would not have been able to accomplish this without the help of her own mother, Chava. Chava was a widow, still sprightly despite her more than sixty years. She cleaned house and took care of her daughter's young children, allowing Gittel the freedom to pursue her real vocation, that of a seamstress. Her work was of high quality, and as a successful businesswoman, Gittel kept abreast of current fashions in catering to her clientele. In so doing, she had been obliged to pick up German and Polish, which she spoke almost as well as her native Yiddish. Most of her clients came from outside Poznan's ghetto, the wives of well-to-do bourgeois tradespeople, most of them with illusions of grandeur that they were partially able to fulfill using their husbands' more than ample income.

Herschel found little in common on the intellectual level with his wife, Gittel. Yet, although their lives seemed to run along parallel lines, those lines intersected through the deep affection they shared for each other, cemented by love for their children. The latter ranged from two to thirteen, the oldest being a girl who did her best to help her hard-working mother and grandmother. Herschel, for his part, tried to supplement the basic knowledge of Judaism his children received at cheder, but there was little else he could discuss with them. So for him, Jonathan's intellectual stimulation was like a gentle summer shower blowing across a parched field.

Herschel realized that he would have to keep his relationship with Jonathan and that with his family strictly apart. He could discern no affinity between the two, and although he told Gittel about his friendship with Jonathan, the thought of inviting him to a Sabbath dinner never occurred to him. Besides, Gittel was too exhausted by the time Friday rolled around to want to exert herself in polite conversation. Nor did Herschel wish to impose his children, not always on their best behavior, on young Jonathan.

His youthful friend also intrigued Herschel by appearing to be so conventional while being so basically different. Herschel understood that Jonathan had no choice in his attraction to men. God had created him that way, so there was no moral judgment to be made. But he wondered whether there was an emotional component to Jonathan's physical desires. He decided to broach the subject with him over one of their regular glasses of tea in the restaurant.

"Jonathan, there's one thing in your past we've never talked about. It's quite personal, so if you prefer not to discuss it, we can drop the subject. Have you, that is, can you love another man, emotionally not just physically?"

Jonathan's eyes clouded over. Velvel flashed into his mind as he suppressed the tears.

Finally, he said, "Yes, Herschel, I can love a man. I loved a man once and he loved me. It was a complete, almost spiritual relationship, like the one you have with Gittel, but obviously without the children."

Herschel waited for Jonathan to continue. "His name was Velvel, and to me, he was everything I could wish for. We were together for about four months only. Then we were discovered. They sent him away, and I… that is why they tried to make me marry."

Herschel said nothing, giving Jonathan the time to recover from his painful memories. Then he said: "Jonathan, you know you can always tell me if I ask too many questions."

Jonathan looked up. "Herschel, you don't understand. There is nobody in this world I can talk to, only you. You can even ask me which shoe I put on first in the morning, and I'll tell you." He laughed at the flippancy of his statement. "Herschel, you are the best thing that has happened to me since Velvel, and I can never thank you enough."

It had been some time since I had ventured to interrupt Jonathan's tale. Yet, at this point in the telling, there was something I had to say.

"In my experience, friendships have usually proven to be much more valuable than loving relationships. When the physical imposes on the emotional, a strain may be placed on the bond of affection, especially if one of the partners is under pressure."

"But isn't love about giving each other support in times of crisis?"

"Yes. But in my world, there is so much freedom to find physical stimulation outside a partnership that commitment and monogamy have become words that have all but lost their meaning. It takes a great deal of self-discipline to remain faithful, as well as a realization that the values of real love, of giving and taking, are worth so much more than a passing thrill. And what I am saying applies to a conventional marriage as well as to relationships between two men or two women."

"In the shtetl, where I came from, infidelity was something we never heard of. Survival depended on sharing responsibilities not only as a couple, but for the sake of the children."

"Unlike today's world," I said. "So many children now have more than one step-parent because their mother or father divorce and remarry, some more than once. Fortunately, that was not my experience. But that is why I say that true friendship, in all but a few cases, is more important than a physical relationship that is not likely to last."

Chapter 8

It was late March. The sun had shone all day leaving the first scent of spring in the air. Jonathan and Herschel strolled through the busy main street of Poznan on their way from the yeshiva to the Pinsky restaurant for their usual evening tea, served in the customary glass. The street was clogged with bustling pedestrians on the boardwalks each side of the street, as well as carts, carriages and horses with their riders, often cavalrymen, clattering on the cobblestone pavement. Jonathan and Hershel were still engaged in the discussion they had begun at the yeshiva on honesty in business and the need for the use of correct weights to measure quantities.

Their conversation was interrupted by distant shouting, increasingly punctuated by women's screams. They turned to face the source of the commotion and saw the road traffic accelerating toward them or detouring into side streets. People were running trying to avoid the disturbance, which proved to be a bolting horse dragging a two-wheel carriage for hire, which bounced along behind the panicking animal. Something had evidently frightened the horse, and the driver was nowhere to be seen. The passengers inside the carriage were a man and a woman, the man's arm stretched across his companion to try and prevent her from being thrown out. The young woman was too terrified even to scream. The careening horse, frothing at the mouth, quickly approached Jonathan and Herschel. Over the pounding hooves and the screaming pedestrians, Hershel shouted to Jonathan: "Cross to the other side and grab the reins there. I'll do the same this side!"

Jonathan quickly crossed the street. As the horse and vehicle drew level with him and with Herschel, they ran alongside it on either side and seized the horse's reins. The two men were yanked off their feet while the horse, surprised at being checked by unseen forces, reared up on its hind legs, then crashed to the ground and slowed to a walk. Jonathan and Herschel kept hold of the reins and walked alongside the frightened animal. Herschel patted the terrified animal's neck and whispered soft words to calm it down. The crisis seemed over, but protruding from the road surface was a loose cobblestone. Hershel's left foot struck it. He stumbled and fell beneath the horse, directly in line with the still advancing left wheel of the carriage. With the hubbub around him, Jonathan had not noticed Herschel's slip and still led the horse forward.

It was Hershel's destiny not to survive the day. He landed on his back and looked up at the horse's belly. He attempted to rise, but the horse, sensing an obstacle blocking its hooves, kicked forward with its hind leg, striking Herschel in the temple and knocking him unconscious. Relentlessly, the wheel of the vehicle rolled forward and then over his chest, crushing his ribs and killing him instantly.

A gasp rose from the watching crowd, initially relieved at the ending of the danger, and then shocked to see one of the heroes killed before their eyes. Jonathan looked over the back of the horse. Hershel had disappeared.

Men dashed from the crowd to assist the prone man, to no avail. His lifeless body was carried to a nearby store. One of the men grabbed the rein from Jonathan who, having realized that Herschel was down and covered in blood, stood motionless in the street in a state of disbelief. Two minutes before, he had been deep in conversation with his only friend. Now he was dead. Jonathan sank to the edge of the boardwalk in shock, sitting on the curb, his head in his hands. His life seemed suspended in mid-air.

A deep voice and a hand on his shoulder brought him back to an indistinct present. "Sir, my sister and I want to thank you."

"What?" Who could be calling him 'sir'?

Jonathan heard a female voice. "We were the passengers. We could have died. You saved our lives."

"My friend… My friend, Herschel, is he alive?"

"We are so sorry. He did not survive," the man said. "It was a terrible accident." He paused, not knowing what to say next. "May I at least help you to get to wherever you were going? A friend of my sister is in the crowd and will accompany her home. Please, let me help you." He held out his hand to help Jonathan rise. "Fanny," he said to his sister, "Larissa is over there. Ask her to take you home, and I'll help this young man to reach his destination."

Jonathan saw the elegant young woman walk toward her similarly dressed friend on the other side of the street. He felt a strong arm around his shoulders.

"Where are you going?"

"To the Pinsky restaurant." Jonathan allowed himself to be supported and led to the restaurant a few blocks away. He was quite unaware of his surroundings, knowing only that he drew some comfort from the strength of the man whom he and Herschel had rescued.

The stranger entered the restaurant and explained what had happened to Abraham Pinsky. Jonathan sat at a table, slumped with his head on his forearm. Mr. Pinsky insisted that Jonathan and the man down a shot of schnapps, which effectively dulled Jonathan's senses. Everything around him appeared blurred. The man thanked Jonathan again, expressed sympathy at his loss and left. Abraham Pinsky helped Jonathan up to his room, laid him on his bed and removed his shoes. That evening he excused Jonathan from his usual performance for the diners in the restaurant.

Abraham Pinsky was also upset at the death of Herschel, Jonathan's best friend. He had a meal prepared for the

Kaufmans that Leibl, his son, took over to the shocked family. For his part, Jonathan had no appetite at all. He remained in his room, dozing and wracked by nightmares in which Herschel appeared sometimes walking backward, with a twisted grin on his face. In other bad dreams, Jonathan's family stood as if posing for a portrait, his sisters and father waving, his mother, crying.

The next morning, fighting fatigue, Jonathan nevertheless went to the yeshiva. He sat in his usual place staring into space, the book in front of him closed. For the third time, his world had ended. First, Velvel; then his family; now Herschel. He was brought back to reality by one of the younger students tapping his shoulder.

"Rabbi Bistrisky would like to see you. Please come with me to his study."

Jonathan followed the youth to the study of the head of the yeshiva.

"Come in Jonathan. Please close the door and sit down." Jonathan sat down facing the rabbi, his face grey from lack of sleep.

"Jonathan, I am so sorry," the rabbi said. "I only wish I could say something to comfort you."

"Why is God doing this to me?" Jonathan whispered, tears trickling from the corner of his eyes.

"Jonathan, we cannot, we must not question the ways of God. He gave you the precious gift of Herschel's knowledge and friendship. Now He has taken it away. It is His right. We must accept it. It's a tragedy, but there's nothing we can do about it. And there is a way you can help your friend Herschel. His three boys have not yet had their bar mitzvah. They are very young. They will need your support, particularly the two oldest. As children, they are not yet required to say the Kaddish but they will probably wish to do so, and I will let you say it with them. We all know how close you and Herschel were. It will give you some comfort."

Jonathan lifted his head. How strange, he thought, that the deep friendship between him and Herschel earned the respect of the rabbi, yet had there been a physical component in their relationship, they would have been roundly condemned. Jonathan felt sympathy for this rabbi, a virtual stranger, who had the unpleasant task of helping him face his loss.

"I thank you, rabbi. Thank you for your kind words. It will be an honor for me to help the boys say Kaddish." He stood. "Forgive me, rabbi. I need to be alone for a while."

Jonathan went into the adjacent shul and sat in one of the pews, his head on his arm resting on the back of the pew in front. His body heaved as he gave vent to his grief. From one moment to the next, my world changes, he thought, from celebration to mourning, from mourning to celebration. And again, we couldn't even say goodbye.

According to Jewish law, burials have to take place within twenty-four hours of death, so the funeral was the next afternoon. Under a heavy sky, Jonathan stood in the cemetery with his arms round the shoulders of Herschel's two older boys, aged ten and twelve. The youngest boy, being only two, stayed at home with his three sisters and his mother – women did not attend funerals. When the time came for the boys to say Kaddish at the graveside, Jonathan intoned the prayer with them, his cheeks streaked with tears, while the two boys did not yet fully comprehend that they would never see their father again.

In the following days, Jonathan dutifully visited the shiva house morning and evening to make up the minyan to say the prayers. Every day, he said the Kaddish with the two older boys. For them, although not obligated, their religious task would be to chant the prayer morning and evening for eleven months to elevate their father's soul toward its divine source. Jonathan shared with them what he regarded as a privilege for the seven-day shiva period only. He also met Herschel's widow, Gittel, a pleasant enough woman; but he understood why Herschel had not wished them to meet. Jonathan had nothing in common with Gittel or the children.

As the shiva came to an end the emotional shock of Herschel's loss struck Jonathan. Once again isolation pervaded his existence. Yet he hardly had time to indulge in any self-pity – his life was too busy. His yeshiva studies and evening performances filled his life. It was mainly at the time of day when they had habitually been alone, between their study sessions and his musical evenings, that he missed his intimate chats with Herschel. How rare it had been to find a man, a normal man with a normal family, who had been so sympathetic to his situation, a situation condemned universally within the ghetto and by society in general! Nevertheless, Jonathan realized that his sexual desires were not unique. There had been one or two occasions when he had noticed different men on the street looking at him and even smiling; but they had been gentiles, and a ghetto Jew could have no contact with non-Jews apart from a business deal.

Despite this convention, two days after the shiva for Herschel ended, Jonathan arrived back at the restaurant to find a sealed note in his room addressed to him. He opened it. The note was written in German, which Jonathan was unable to read. For although he could understand the language thanks to its close linguistic affinity with Yiddish, the language of the Jews was written in Hebrew script, not in German characters. He therefore asked Pessie, the Pinsky's oldest child, to read it to him since she had learned to read the language at school. Seated across the table from Jonathan in the restaurant, she read to him in her very best German, carefully enunciating each word without even trying to understand its meaning.

Dear Mr. Brodski,

They told me your name when I revisited the restaurant a few days ago when you were out. My sister, Fanny, and I want to thank you again for

> *having so courageously rescued us from what would certainly have been a most serious accident. I also wish to express my heartfelt sympathy to you on the loss of your dear friend Herschel. I have sent a similar note to his family.*
>
> *I understand that you are available at the restaurant in the early evening. With your permission, I shall pass by tomorrow to see you. I would like to offer you a more tangible expression of our deep gratitude.*

The letter was signed Hermann von Stahlberg.

Jonathan thanked Pessie for her effort and remained seated in the empty restaurant. He was dumbfounded. He did not feel that he and Herschel had done anything heroic. They had reacted instinctively. The horse had not seemed to be galloping so fast. In fact, it had seemed to be slowing down when they brought it to a halt. Nevertheless, Jonathan was intrigued by the apparent concern of Hermann von Stahlberg, and by the prospect of meeting someone so different from the people he usually frequented.

In the late afternoon of the following day, on returning from the yeshiva, Jonathan approached the restaurant to find a small group of boys outside, their faces pressed up against the window.

"What is it?" he asked. "What are you looking at?"

One of the boys said, "There's a Prussian officer in there... In our restaurant!"

"Be off with you," said Jonathan roughly. "A Prussian officer is not a show. Leave him in peace." The boys ran off laughing.

Jonathan entered the restaurant, at that hour empty of diners. He saw a tall-looking man with light brown hair sitting with his back to the entrance, doubtless to avoid the stares of the Jewish boys at the window. On the chair beside him was the spiked helmet of his regiment, partly covered by his greatcoat. He wore the dark blue tunic of his unit, white breeches and high black boots. There could be no doubt that this was Hermann von Stahlberg, probably the first such patron to visit the kosher restaurant.

"Herr von Stahlberg," Jonathan said.

The man turned around and stood. He was about six feet tall and appeared to be in his late twenties. He clicked his heels and bowed slightly.

"Mr. Brodski, I am honored to meet you again under slightly less harrowing circumstances." The voice was deep and the language was High German. He smiled. Jonathan noticed his clean-cut face, his finely shaped mouth, the steely blue eyes and the refined sculpture of his eyebrows. The man was undoubtedly handsome. Jonathan held out his hand, which was grasped in von Stahlberg's strong grip.

"May I offer you a glass of tea?" Jonathan asked. His Yiddish, a dialect of Low German, was easily understood by the Prussian officer.

"Thank you."

Hot water was constantly simmering in the samovar in the kitchen and Jonathan soon returned with two steaming glasses of tea.

With Jonathan seated once again at the table, von Stahlberg said, "Mr. Brodski, mere words were not enough for my sister and me to thank you for your bravery and sacrifice, so I have brought you a small token of our gratitude." He reached into a deep inner pocket of his coat and pulled out a package wrapped in brown paper bound with a fine silk red ribbon.

"The ribbon was my sister's, Fanny's idea." His smiling eyes looked at Jonathan, who was not quite sure how to react. "Won't you open it?"

Jonathan held the gift in his hand and looked at the delicate wrapping. A feeling of guilt engulfed him. Here he was, accepting what could be considered a reward, while

Herschel, the person whom he had loved and respected more than anyone else in the world (apart from Velvel), lay dead and buried in the ground. His eyes glistened with tears.

"But I cannot accept this, Herr von Stahlberg. My friend, my best friend, Herschel is dead, so how can I take pleasure from his loss? What right do I have to profit from his death?"

It was Hermann von Stahlberg's turn to be dismayed.

"I understand, Mr. Brodski. But if Herschel were here now, do you think he would begrudge you this gift. You and he saved our lives. We cannot show him our gratitude, but we can express it to you. Both Fanny and I will be so disappointed if you refuse to accept our small gift. It is our only way of thanking you and thanking Herschel, through you, for your bravery."

Jonathan contemplated the package again. Herschel, with his vast interest in all human activity, would surely not have refused this token of thanks. Jonathan slowly untied the ribbon and carefully unwrapped the gift, trying not to tear the paper. Somehow, the process was as precious as the present itself. The package consisted of a framed picture, delicately painted in oils, depicting the details of a brick mansion set among lush lawns surrounded by trees. It was something that Jonathan had never seen before.

"A painting..." He paused, examining every detail. "Where is this place?"

"It's my family home in Mecklenburg. I painted it several years ago and brought it with me when I was posted to Posen," he said, referring to the city's German name. "My sister is visiting me for a few days and will return home shortly. Do you like our little gift?"

Jonathan looked at the framed view again. "I have never seen anything so beautiful before." Indeed, apart from one or two pictures that Jonathan had glimpsed through the windows of homes in the city and a few biblical scenes painted on panels in shuls, this was the first painting that Jonathan had ever seen, not to mention the first he had ever held in his hands.

Paintings of secular subjects, such as this landscape, were considered a forbidden luxury, *avoda zora,* leading to the temptation of idol worship. But, thought Jonathan, how could admiring a depiction of man's God-given creative genius lead to idol worship? Jonathan smiled at the work of art in appreciation.

"It is something you richly deserve," said Hermann. "I'm delighted that you like it. Now, whenever you look at it, you will remember how brave you were and how eternally grateful we are. And I will always remember the expression on your face when you accepted our small gift."

Jonathan looked up and smiled, self-consciously. "The expression on my face?"

"Yes, Jonathan. May I call you Jonathan?"

"Of course."

"Jonathan, although I am a military officer, I am also something of a painter. I appreciate what is beautiful in the world, perhaps to offset some of the ugliness I see every day. And seeing your face, your surprise, your joy, is a beautiful thing to me."

Jonathan was taken aback. "Me? Beautiful?"

"Forgive me. Perhaps I have been too bold. I don't wish to offend."

Jonathan repeated the word in his head. Beautiful. Could a man be beautiful? He had never considered the concept. Naomi had been beautiful, both inside and out. But a man? He looked again at Hermann von Stahlberg, this time in a new light. If a woman could be beautiful, why not a man? And this one, Jonathan thought, was most certainly beautiful. He decided that he had nothing to lose.

"Perhaps… Perhaps you are beautiful, too," he said tentatively as the color rushed to his cheeks. Had he just said that?

Von Stahlberg leaned back in his chair and let out a deep laugh. "So, we are both beautiful! Now I can relax a little, and so can you." He put his hand into his tunic pocket and took out a matchbox and a silver case from which he extracted a cigarillo. He lit up, stretching his long legs underneath the table.

"I suspect this restaurant has never seen a meeting such as ours."

"It's true. Not many Prussian officers come to eat here." Jonathan smiled and looked again at his picture. "It is so very beautiful. I shall treasure it."

"Strange, a Jewish man who appreciates art. Of course, why not?" It was his turn to smile. "What else do you appreciate, Jonathan?"

"Well, Herr von…"

"Please, call me Hermann."

"Well, Hermann, I love music. In fact, I am a violinist and I play here every evening, in the Pinsky restaurant."

"How I would love to hear you play, but I fear my presence would be somewhat intimidating to the other diners. What sort of music do you play?"

"Jewish music, of course. But my friend Herschel… Oh…" His eyes flooded with tears as he reminisced about his lost friend. Hermann's brow furrowed with concern. His hand went instinctively to hold Jonathan's, resting on the table.

"I'm so sorry. I didn't mean to bring back memories of Herschel. I'd like to help you recover from his loss."

"Herschel was one of the most understanding men I've ever met. He was also one of the brightest, interested in everything and everyone. I shall never forget him."

"I'm sorry I was not privileged to know him myself," said Hermann. "And I'm so sorry his absence is causing you such pain."

Jonathan felt the Prussian officer's warm hand on his own and withdrew.

"My touching you… Does it embarrass you?" asked the Prussian.

"Here, in the restaurant… Even if there's no one around… Yes…" Jonathan wiped his cheeks with the back of his hand.

"But if we were somewhere else, somewhere private?"

Jonathan looked at him and then looked away. Hermann said nothing. Jonathan turned back and looked intently into Hermann's eyes, blue like an endless sky.

"No," he said softly. "I would not be embarrassed."

"Then we should arrange to meet again, elsewhere."

Jonathan blushed. "You mean that you want to see me again?"

"Yes, that is what I'm trying to say." Hermann laughed.

"Where? How?" The notion of meeting a Prussian officer in public made Jonathan panic. They would indeed make an incongruous couple, a Jewish man in traditional dress and a Prussian officer in uniform.

"Jonathan, I know that we cannot be seen together. Today, I have a valid excuse for speaking to you. But in the future..." He stubbed out his cigarillo. "However, I have a suggestion for you. We could meet by the band shell in the park and at least take a walk through the trees."

"Yes, we could. But when?"

"Sunday evening at about this time, after your school. What do you call it?"

"Yeshiva."

"Yes, yeshiva. Can you be free then? We'll write a book together and call it 'The Yeshiva and the Barracks'." He stood as he joked.

"Yes, I can be there."

"Now I must go and attend to my duties. I'll see you on Sunday."

Jonathan rose to his feet and held out his hand. Hermann took it in both of his and squeezed firmly. "You won't change your mind, will you?"

"I won't change my mind."

Hermann von Stahlberg threw his greatcoat over his shoulders. He picked up his helmet from the chair beside him, drew his gloves over his finely chiseled hands, clicked his heels and left.

Jonathan sat down again and cradled what was left of his cold tea in his hands. He looked again at Hermann's picture lying on the table. Beautiful, he said to himself, thinking more of the artist than the art. He could hardly believe the sudden surge of hope in his breast, a hope mixed with desire. But where could this lead? Their lives were worlds apart. Even the language they spoke was different. His hopes crashed. But then, he thought, why look to the future? Sunday was only four days away. He could allow himself the luxury of hope until Sunday. Nothing could replace drinking tea with Herschel, but a walk with Hermann might prove to be second best.

Chapter 9

Over the intervening days, Jonathan's feelings of hope were mixed with moments of anxiety and despair. He felt that he could share nothing more with this Prussian officer than his picture. He placed it on the chest of drawers in his room and looked at it constantly, imagining an elegant Prussian lady – perhaps Fanny – playing the piano behind one of the windows in the house, or aristocratic Prussian officers playing cards and smoking behind another. Then he pictured them at dinner, at a long table set with crystal wine glasses, fine porcelain and candles. But how could he himself ever fit into that unfamiliar setting, and how could he eat the non-kosher food they were eating? Never. So why even hope?

Jonathan realized that not only would any possible physical relationship between him and Hermann be condemned according to the social norms of the day, but so would their very friendship. He and Hermann would not even be able to walk down the street together. A Jew and an army officer could never do that, barring an unpleasant incident.

Sitting in shul on the shabbes morning before his tryst the next day with Hermann, he mused on the path this new connection might take. The concentration of some other worshipers, likewise preoccupied by their own problems, had drifted away from their immediate surroundings. They were all jolted back to reality by a sudden swelling in the voice of the cantor, vaunting his musical prowess. "Why can't he just maintain his usual monotone?" thought Jonathan, irritated by the interruption. "He just wants to be noticed and not ignored," he muttered under his breath.

Unprepared as Jonathan was for his meeting with the Prussian officer, the set time arrived. He made his way through the streets of Poznan to the park near the city center, his heart pounding, his breath short. Dusk was falling as the band shell came into view on a small rise in the center of the park. Hermann was standing nearby, smoking. His helmet was on the grass beside him and he was wearing his greatcoat.

"You came," he said. "I wasn't sure you would."

"I promised. I wouldn't let you down."

This time, they did not shake hands and Hermann did not click his heels.

"Let's take a walk," Hermann said. He picked up his helmet and the two men made their way along a gravel path leading to the shelter of the nearby trees.

"I've been thinking a lot about you, Jonathan. In fact, I missed you."

Jonathan said nothing. He was very nervous. As they walked their hands touched, it seemed again and again.

"I have been thinking, too. I am confused."

"Confused? Why?"

They had reached a part of the woodland where the trees were quite thick. Nobody could see them from the band shell nor from the more distant street.

"I want so much to be a friend of yours. But how can that be possible?"

The question remained unanswered. Hermann leaned back against a tree and unbuttoned his greatcoat. "Come here, Jonathan." He held out his arms. Jonathan turned to face him and gently inclined his body into Hermann's. He felt like the dove Noah sent from the ark after the great flood to seek dry land, returning with an olive leaf in its beak. Jonathan took a deep breath as Hermann wrapped his coat around him. Hermann had a special aroma about him, a blend of cigar smoke and cologne. They stood motionless, savoring the experience of total peace.

"You are a beautiful man, Jonathan." Hermann removed Jonathan's cap and kissed his hair. Jonathan snuggled closer.

"I want to see your eyes," Jonathan said. Hermann looked down at Jonathan who could barely make out their rich tint of blue as the failing light spread through the woods. "Let me kiss them." Hermann tilted his head, which Jonathan held between his hands before gently kissing his eyes. Hermann then placed his hands on Jonathan's cheeks and kissed him gently on the lips.

Jonathan's arousal was instantaneous and before he could control himself, he reached a climax and soiled himself.

"Gevalt!" he muttered. "I'm sorry," he said. "I couldn't help it."

A quiet laugh escaped Hermann's lips. Then he guffawed. "So, Jonathan, you do find me attractive!" Jonathan laughed at the obvious remark and laughed again, partly out of relief.

"Well, perhaps I do."

"We'll have to practice this and get it right next time."

For the following few Sundays, Jonathan and Hermann met again by the band shell and wandered off into the woods. Jonathan reveled in the pure physical release of making love with a handsome man whom he could trust and with whom he could relax. Both men were equally at risk and both understood that the relationship could neither move forward nor become permanent. For Jonathan, his relationship with Hermann held none of the music, magic or mutual spirituality he had shared with Velvel. For Hermann, intent on pursuing his military career, the thought of more than a sexual relationship with Jonathan never crossed his mind. Indeed, he had firmly resolved to force himself to marry at some point in the future, purely to further his career and to meet his family's expectations of him. Not that marriage would ever prevent him from having dalliances on the side with men. He would never have considered questioning the way things were done in his circumstances and in his social circle.

Nevertheless, from its purely sexual beginnings, a friendship slowly emerged. Jonathan and Hermann talked to each other, each curious about the other's radically different lifestyle. Jonathan completely shattered the preconceived prejudices Hermann held against Jews. How could a Jew have brought a bolting horse to a halt? How could a Jew, Herschel, have lost his life in possibly saving his? And as he slowly learned more about Jonathan's studies and his Jewish heritage, a new respect for Judaism took root in Hermann's psyche. Of course, he thought, Jewish culture could never be compared to that of German-speaking people with their abundant stock of literature and music, yet Hermann recognized the richness of a philosophy that reached back many centuries.

Jonathan, on the other hand, while he appreciated the attention he received from Hermann and the latter's curiosity about his life, could find little to admire in Hermann's philosophy and way of life. Hermann von Stahlberg had been born into a privileged class of minor landed gentry in the Grand Duchy of Mecklenburg and, as the second son in a family of four boys, had joined the Prussian army. He was very aware of his rank as a lieutenant in the Hussars, and he held in the utmost contempt the common conscripts under his command who survived in appalling conditions. His favorite pastime was hunting for deer in the forests of his home estate, as well as target practice using his regulation rifle. However, he had a fine sensitivity for music by German composers, especially Schubert, and he naturally appreciated the works of European artists, having made frequent visits to Paris and Rome. However, his favorite artist, whose works he had seen on exhibition in Dresden, was the Romantic painter Caspar David Friedrich, a compatriot. To complement his artistic interests, Hermann was also well versed in the writings of Heinrich Heine, a man whom he knew had been born Jewish but who had converted to Christianity.

Jonathan looked forward to hearing about Hermann's travels and the artistic wonders he had seen and heard, but he relegated Hermann's other preoccupations to the back of his mind. It was no wonder that his relationship with Hermann was so different from that with Velvel. The two men could hardly be compared. Hermann was far better looking than Velvel, more impressive and more worldly. But Jonathan realized that the two components lacking in his friendship with Hermann and which had been so evident in his relationship with Velvel were mutual commitment and a shared spirituality. Indeed, the word *friendship* was one Jonathan would never have applied to what he had felt for Velvel. He unashamedly admitted to himself that what he had felt for Velvel was love; what he felt for Hermann was friendship mixed with a measure of curiosity about a lifestyle with which he was totally unfamiliar and which he would never experience.

As the season advanced, the days grew longer. Without the sheltering cover of darkness, Jonathan and Hermann feared discovery if they should continue their illicit physical relationship in daylight, even deep in the woods of the park. Nevertheless, they still met in the late afternoon for the pleasure of each other's company, exploring worlds unfamiliar to them both.

One Sunday, Jonathan wandered toward the band shell. His thoughts flowed in an unrelated stream – his studies of the day at the yeshiva, how his life seemed to be falling into place, and thankfulness for the spiritual tranquility he had come close to achieving. As he strolled along the gravel path, he became aware of footsteps behind him, the footsteps of more than one person. He hastened his pace, fearful of looking back. The crunch of boots on the gravel speeded up, faster than his. A voice called in Polish: "Hey, Jewboy, you did it! You killed our lord, didn't you!"

Jonathan's heart raced. To this point in his life, he had avoided any anti-Jewish incident. Now his luck had apparently run out.

"Did you enjoy hammering in the nails?" another voice cried.

Jonathan continued walking, saying nothing. The footsteps drew closer. A rough hand seized Jonathan's arm spinning him round. Facing him were three teenage thugs.

"So," said the tallest one, "how does it feel to be a murderer? And how many Christian kids does your mother need to bake her bread?"

At the mention of his mother, Jonathan's own blood boiled. He raised his fists.

"Come on then, *momzerim,* bastards. Give me your worst!"

The three louts hesitated. They were unaccustomed to a Jew offering resistance. Then they cast their gaze beyond Jonathan. Strolling down the pathway was a tall Prussian officer. Reluctant to cause a scene that might trigger a formal investigation, the would-be attackers backed off, turned tail and ran back down the path.

"Are you alright, Jonathan?" asked Hermann. "I saw what was going on from the band shell."

"Yes, I think so," said Jonathan. "You arrived just in time."

"They know no better. Ignorant kids that they are."

"That's all they are now. Later, when they've grown up, they'll become murderers themselves."

The two men made their way up toward the band shell and beyond it to the woods, Hermann feeling guilty about the un-Christian behavior of the so-called Christian youths, and Jonathan feeling partly resentful and partly relieved about the unpleasant incident.

After several weeks, circumstances arose that presented both a problem and a solution to their restricted relationship. Hermann von Stahlberg had been stationed in Poznan for two years. He was offered a promotion to the rank of captain with a sister regiment that was to take up position on the French frontier – the Franco-Prussian War of 1870 was about to erupt. No thought ever crossed Hermann von Stahlberg's mind of sacrificing his career to build a life with Jonathan Brodski, and bearing the social ostracism that such a decision would bring.

At their next meeting, he said: "Jonathan, I have something to tell you. I hope it will not hurt you too much."

Jonathan knew instinctively that it was the end. "What is it, or can I guess?" He wondered what excuse Hermann would give him.

"I have to go away. I am to be stationed first in Königsberg, and then we'll move west."

Jonathan felt a mixture of fear, relief and regret. Hermann had explained the political situation on the French border to Jonathan, who recognized the potential danger of Hermann's move. However, the strain of having to find excuses for his late arrival at the restaurant every Sunday had been difficult and, although he had grown used to enjoying what had become mainly intellectual contact with Hermann, clearly their relationship could go nowhere. But the prospect of returning to his lonely existence was daunting.

"Must you leave? Do you have any choice in the matter?" Jonathan asked, knowing full well what the answer would be.

"No, Jonathan, I have no choice. I'm due to leave in two weeks."

"I am sorry you're going. I never imagined I would have the chance to meet anyone like you. I will miss you deeply."

"It's for the best. I will miss you, too. I have learned so much about your people and your religion. It's been… It's been…" He searched for the appropriate word. "It's truly been a blessing, Jonathan. I shall also be forever in your debt for rescuing my sister and me. At least you have my painting to remind you of that and of our good times together."

Jonathan hugged him, clinging tightly. "I will never forget you. And remember, you rescued me, too."

Two weeks later, they parted, each realizing that they would never see the other again. Hermann was on his way to furthering his military career, while Jonathan, less driven and less directed, returned to his relatively isolated routine, accepting once again his lack of physical fulfillment or emotional attachment.

Inevitably his thoughts turned to the people he missed most. In his moments alone, in his room, during the walks he occasionally took on a Friday afternoon or on the way back to the restaurant from the yeshiva, Hermann, Herschel and Velvel loomed up in his imagination. He could not even dispel the importunate images of his family, his Tatteh, his Mommeh, Rivkeleh and Estherel, and together, they deepened his sadness. There seemed to be nobody in his present life that could come close to replacing the love he felt for each of them in different ways.

At this low point in Jonathan's emotional fortunes he suffered another blow. At the entrance to the yeshiva was a notice board that served as a community newspaper. To it were pinned notices of births, deaths and marriages and any other announcements of concern to the local Jewish community. One morning, as Jonathan entered the study hall, his eye was caught by a prominent poster lined with a double black border. It was a cherem circulated to all institutions of higher learning and shuls stating the terms of an individual's excommunication and signed by the rabbi responsible. And there, for all to see was the name Yankl Bradawka over the name of Rabbi Levy. The details of the miscreant's sin were not mentioned in the notice, probably for fear of indirectly encouraging some misguided individual to copy the crime.

Jonathan's first reaction was one of shock. So this was Rabbi Levy's revenge for his having left the shtetl. His own self-imposed exile was not enough. The learned rabbi had tried to destroy him completely. No support, no contact, no communication with any other Jew. His second reaction was the shame this must have caused to his dear parents. Yet he remembered having written to them that he had changed his name, so the effect of the decree would be nullified.

Nevertheless, not having received any response from his mother or father, he could not be sure that they had ever received his letter. But the cherem might explain this absence of communication. He laughed sardonically to himself. Rabbi Levy could excommunicate Yankl Bradawka as much as he liked, but that name had ceased to exist when he had quit his native village. Jonathan shrugged as he entered the study hall.

"I am constantly reminded of the similarity between anti-Semitism and what we today call homophobia," I explained to Jonathan, "the hatred shown toward men or women who love those of their own sex. Both forms of prejudice are based on what people don't know, don't understand and don't want to understand."

"Yes. I suppose that is the very nature of prejudice," Jonathan responded. "For me, anti-Semitism was a reality I had to live with. But I could only avoid people's condemnation of my natural affection for other men by leaving or disguising my true feelings."

"Yes, that's quite clear from the incident with the anti-Semitic young thugs by the band shell. Only Hermann's presence averted a dangerous outcome, and the action of Rabbi Levy in pronouncing the cherem against you because of your love for Velvel."

"Exactly. And you," said Jonathan, "have you ever suffered a similar experience?"

"Indeed I have, and both anti-Semitism and homophobia were combined in the same monstrous individual. I was living with my lover, Yves, here in Montreal, in a house that we had carefully restored to its original beauty."

"You lived with a man?" asked Jonathan, incredulous. "A lover? You lived openly in a house that you bought together?"

"Yes," I said. "Much of the world, or at least the western world, has evolved. Discrimination against people on the basis of their sexual orientation – whether they are attracted to those of the same sex or the opposite sex – is now illegal in Canada. So much has changed since your times. Couples of the same sex can now not only marry but even adopt children."

"So there are still miracles," exclaimed Jonathan, "even in modern times. It is quite hard for me to imagine. Life must be so easy and good for you. No more secrets, no more hiding and no more running away."

"Up to a certain point," I replied. "But discrimination can still worm its way out through violence. Let me tell you a true story. Two doors away from our house lived a hateful man, Oscar, who was both homophobic and anti-Semitic. He lived on the ground floor of a duplex, a house with two apartments, one above the other. On the upper floor lived an elderly Jewish couple whose daughter was the owner of the duplex. She resided in one of the states in the United States of America, California. Oscar and the old Jewish couple hated each other.

"Once, when Yves and I returned home after a vacation, we found out that the old Jewish lady had died of a heart attack following a screaming argument she'd had with Oscar.

"Oscar bred and sold dogs illegally in his basement, and he also kept a large dog, a German Shepherd, that he tied up in his backyard at night. If anything moved, even leaves blown by the wind, the dog would bark, disturbing our sleep. On two occasions, we called the police to complain about the nighttime barking. They must have given Oscar warnings.

"One day, I was gardening in the front yard, when Oscar passed by. We used to chat, but this time, he interrupted our conversation: 'I know it was you and your friend who called the police. So if I ever see either of you in the back lane, I'll shoot you.' I assumed he had a gun.

"After this death threat, I immediately called the police. They said they could do nothing since no crime had been committed. They couldn't even give the man a warning. They were quite useless. The next day, when we returned from work, one of our windows was broken."

Jonathan leaned back in his armchair. "Violence. All they know is violence. Was that the end of the affair?"

"No. Two months later, at 2:00 in the morning, a rock smashed through my bedroom window. I was in shock. Again, we called the police, but we could prove nothing, and they did nothing. At that

point, I told Yves that, if it happened again, he could have the house, but I would move out.

"Strangely enough, Yves seemed quite nonchalant about the incident. Perhaps he was too attached to the house to acknowledge the absolute hatred that motivated the violence. I, however, was traumatized. I lost my appetite for food and at night, I would lie in my bed, devising schemes to take revenge that I knew I would never carry out. I hated myself for my cowardice and inaction. My thoughts churned back to all the windows that had been broken in pogroms in Russia and Poland, not to mention what happened later in history. And I felt powerless. But vengeance was to come through the hand of God."

"How so?" asked Jonathan, intrigued.

"I'll finish the story. One year later, we went away for a weekend. On our return, we found another window broken. I was white with anger. I took the telephone and dialed our neighbor's number. I knew what I had to say, but I was not prepared for his little girl to answer the phone. Without thinking, I blurted out, 'We're coming to get you.' That was all I said. I never intended to say those words to a little girl.

"Oscar must have gotten the message. He did not venture out of his house for ten days. But we, or should I say I, decided to sell the house and move. Yves was heartbroken. We had put so much love and energy into restoring our home, and he adored it. But, thank God, he cared more for me than for the house, and for that I was eternally grateful to him.

"My evil neighbor persuaded the man who lived in the house between our two homes to make an offer on our house. It was the same amount as we had paid for it, in spite of the increase in market value and the work we had invested in it. We just ignored his offer, especially when, soon after, we received a far better one, which happened to come also from two men who were a couple!

"We moved out and thought that we would hear no more of Oscar. But we did, and this is where the hand of God intervened. After several years, I moved alone to…"

I hesitated in recounting my story. In fact, I had moved to Israel. But how could I explain Israel to Jonathan? Already, describing the altered circumstances of gay people had given him culture shock. Israel, the land we Jews prayed for over so many centuries, has been a reality for so many decades. However, it was so far removed from anything Jonathan could conceive of that I felt I could not impose the idea of it on him. It would be too devastating for him to bear. Furthermore, it would detract from the point of my story. I continued.

"I moved alone to another country. The reasons are not important. Anyway, I was away for about two years, and then I returned to Montreal. On my first shabbes home, I had arranged for the local newspaper to be delivered. And – something I had never done before – I read the obituaries, the death notices. There, before my eyes was an announcement placed by Oscar's wife commemorating his death two years previously." I paused.

"Unbelievable," said Jonathan.

"Yes, completely. It goes beyond coincidence that, for the first time in my life, I should read that part of the newspaper and see that notice. Also, for the first time in my life, I raced around the house, shouting and rejoicing that fate had taken that despicable character off the face of the earth. It confirmed my faith and my belief in divine justice."

"I understand perfectly. I, too, when I look back over my own story, never lost my confidence in divine providence – the gift for music I was born with, and how it helped me survive and make a success of my life. It was as if I had a guardian angel. How could I have managed without it?"

Chapter 10

At the Pinsky home, frequent letters arrived from their son, Benny, in New York. Following in the family tradition, he was now employed in a kosher restaurant on the Lower East Side, the Jewish immigrant area of Manhattan. Within a short time, he had been promoted from waiter to manager, and the restaurant was thriving. Benny had a good business head, and an eye for profitable opportunities. In addition, there was a spirit of freedom in New York that was totally absent in Eastern Europe. The Jews did not live in fear of prejudice and persecution. It was a new country and the possibilities were endless.

About a year after he had emigrated, Benny wrote to his father, Abraham, and suggested that he sell the house and restaurant in Poznan and move with his family to New York. On arriving, Abraham would have enough money to rent an apartment and restaurant premises in New York.

Abraham pondered the proposal. True, he would have to learn English, but Benny already had a working knowledge of the language and would act as a buffer between him and the outside community. It would mean a great upheaval and probably abandoning his elder daughter, Milly, and her family in Poznan. But what a future there would be for Pessie and Leibl! He discussed the move with his wife, Fraidl, who was immediately in favor of starting over again in the New World.

"Abraham, we and the children will be American," she said proudly.

"Yes, my dear. But we'll also lose Milly and her children."

"Not necessarily. Perhaps they'll join us later. We're still not so old. I'm sure you'll soon earn enough money to bring them over."

"Then there's Jonathan. I'll have to break the news to Jonathan."

"He'll be all right. He can stay on and play his violin for the new owners. Yes, that will actually be something extra we can offer them." Despite the kindness of the Pinsky family toward Jonathan, he was still an employee and not an adopted son of the family. After all, thought the Pinskys, he had been married and widowed and would doubtless want to start a new family of his own at some point.

Spring spread its warmth and colors over the country as Abraham Pinsky advertised his house and restaurant for sale. He made the place look as attractive as possible, planting pretty flowers in window boxes below the sills and in large tubs at the entrance. The establishment was well known in the Jewish neighborhood of Poznan, and one or two offers were quickly submitted for consideration. Within a month, the deal was done. The Pinsky family would leave at the end of the summer, enabling them to put aside more money for their forthcoming venture, and the new owners, the Kowalskis, would then take over.

Jonathan accepted the news with equanimity. Although he felt great affection for the family, he realized that, as an employee and as a lodger, he was not a part of it. He had some misgivings about the new owners, hoping they would be as easy to get along with as the Pinskys, but ultimately, he had no choice. His living quarters and his livelihood would be dependent on the new owners, for the present.

In September, a month before the Jewish High Holy Days, the Pinskys left to join their son, Benny, in New York.

Abraham Pinsky bade Jonathan goodbye.

"If you ever decide to come to New York, Jonathan," he said, "come and see us. You could even stay with us for a few days until you get settled. There'll always be a place for you and your violin in my restaurant."

Jonathan considered the possibility seriously. Perhaps people thought differently in America. But two considerations made him put emigration out of his mind. Firstly, in practical terms, he had saved a mere fraction of the cost of passage on a ship to New York. The Pinskys had sold their home and restaurant and with that money in hand, they would be able to afford both the trans-Atlantic tickets and the rental of an apartment and a business. Also, Jonathan realized that, on arriving in New York, he would still be living in a ghetto, albeit a ghetto by choice. And he spoke not one word of English. He did not have the luxury of a son who had preceded him and integrated enough into a new land to smooth the way for him. Thus, his decision to remain in Poznan was virtually predetermined.

The Kowalski family moved in. Abraham Pinsky had been kind enough to insert Jonathan's terms of employment and living conditions into the deed of sale, so he was secure, at least for the time being.

Mottl Kowalski was a middle-aged, burly man, but a natural frown on his face prevented him from appearing as welcoming and friendly as Abraham Pinsky. Nevertheless, he was not unkind and, realizing that Jonathan represented a significant asset to his business, he made sure to treat him with respect. He had previously traveled the country selling furs to wealthy Jews and non-Jews, and now, having saved much of his profits, he wanted to settle down. His wife, Ruth, was an efficient housewife but uncommunicative. She provided Jonathan with his meals in the company of members of her family but showed no interest in his general welfare. Then there were the four children. The youngest, Itsik, was seven, Anshel was nine, Wolf was twelve and Sorele, the oldest was seventeen.

In order to get into the family's good books, on the eve of their first Sabbath in their new home, Jonathan bought a small bunch of flowers. His gift, offered to Mrs. Kowalski in the kitchen, was accepted by her with a nod, more surly than sweet, but by a warm smile from Sorele who was helping her mother prepare the Sabbath meal.

"What beautiful flowers," said Sorele. "Thank you so much!" Her enthusiasm was more worthy of a giant floral centerpiece than of Jonathan's small posy. Jonathan blushed with pleasure.

"It's nothing," he said, "just a small gesture to welcome you all."

"Yes, thank you, Jonathan," said Ruth Kowalski, her daughter's response having obliged her to acknowledge the gift. "Sorele, put them in water," she ordered. "Then slice the onions."

Jonathan quickly adapted to the new family. Mr. Kowalski asked him to spend some time coaching Wolf to chant the Torah portion for his bar mitzvah, a proposal that Jonathan willingly accepted for the extra pay. His lessons filled the time he had formerly passed with Herschel and to a lesser extent with Hermann, providing Jonathan with a welcome distraction from brooding on times past.

Wolf was an enthusiastic student although overly curious.

"Are you married, Mr. Brodski?" he asked.

Jonathan was not used to being addressed by his family name, but being almost ten years older than the boy, he accepted it as inevitable.

"I was, Wolf," said Jonathan tersely.

"What do you mean 'you were'?"

"My wife died."

"Oh," said Wolf. "All right. Yes, all right," he said, embarrassed and at a loss to come up with any more appropriate expression of sympathy.

The boy's confusion served to distract Jonathan from his own discomfort at having to lie. Being dishonest, even with this child, went strongly against his nature although, when he gave it some thought, his entire life was a lie. He was masquerading as a run-of-the-mill man, with 'normal' desires and ambitions – ultimately, a wife, children, a family. Indeed, he would have wanted nothing more, if only he were physically capable. In his present circumstances, he had no choice but to maintain the pretense.

Wolf's bar mitzvah was an occasion for great rejoicing, especially since he was the oldest boy in the family. He chanted his Torah portion with aplomb. At the kiddush, the reception following the shabbes morning service, preceded by the blessing over wine, he delivered a *d'var Torah,* a short talk on a religious subject, composed principally by Jonathan. Although Wolf accepted the adulation of the men in the community following his presentation, Jonathan drew some satisfaction from the acknowledgement the boy had given him at the end of his talk. Mottl Kowalski, Wolf's father, also thanked Jonathan, helping him to put his life into a more realistic perspective. He might be living a lie, but that lie was merely an expedient, and at least it enabled him to make a solid contribution to his community. Jonathan realized, too, how much pleasure his evening performances gave to the restaurant patrons who heard him play. Although incapable of becoming a father, he could nevertheless justify his existence in other ways.

His life fell into a comfortable routine. He forced himself to concentrate on his studies at the yeshiva and blocked out any expectations of ever meeting a chevrusa who would become a kindred spirit. And since all the students at the kollel where he studied were married men, there was little chance of his meeting anyone like himself. In the evenings, he played his violin to the crowd of diners, never prolonging his performance beyond what he thought they would tolerate. After all, they were there to enjoy the company as well as the music. On Friday evenings, when the restaurant was closed, he would join the Kowalski family for the shabbes dinner.

It was at those shabbes dinners with the family that Jonathan became aware of a situation that went beyond coincidence. Since the Kowalskis invariably invited guests to this special meal, the children had no set places at the table. However, it seemed that Sorele, the only girl in the family, was always seated either next to him or facing him. This continued week after week. Jonathan would often look up from his plate to see Sorele smiling at him, or she would frequently ask him if he would like a second helping.

Jonathan tried to ignore Sorele's obvious interest in him. But one shabbes, after lunch, Wolf asked him to take a walk with him. Jonathan agreed.

"Can Sorele come too?" asked Wolf.

"Of course," said Jonathan, unable to refuse.

Winter had passed and spring had come early to Poznan. The sun shone brightly as they left the apartment above the restaurant. Wolf and Jonathan had exchanged their shtreimels for their usual peaked caps. Sorele wore a skirt that came down to her ankles and a long-sleeved blouse with a flower pattern on a white background. With her long brown hair, sparkling eyes and red lips, she looked very pretty.

The three young people walked through the ghetto streets with only a few strollers out enjoying the weather. They reached a park not far from the city center. It was the same park with the band shell where Jonathan had enjoyed his secret rendez-vous with Hermann. He looked wistfully up the sloping grass to the woods beyond, where they had shared their moments of passion and talk. He cast the memory out of his mind. It was a relationship that, from the outset, was destined to come to an end, and now was not the time to be thinking of it.

The trio chatted easily, the boys discussing what they were currently studying, and joking with Sorele about the elderly guests the Kowalskis had entertained the previous evening. They poked gentle fun at the couple, without being malicious. The conversation then turned to more personal topics.

"Wolf tells me you've been married," Sorele said to Jonathan.

"Yes, I have. For a time, I was very happy." Jonathan again thought of Velvel, and then, guiltily, of Naomi.

"I was so sorry to hear about your wife," Sorele added. "Perhaps, one day, you'll marry again, and be happy again."

"Perhaps one day," Jonathan said noncommittally.

"But you would like to get married, wouldn't you?" Sorele persisted.

Anxious not to let down his guard, Jonathan said: "Of course I would."

Wolf interjected. "I want to get married before I'm twenty. But perhaps I'll learn a trade so that I can have lots of children and my wife can take care of them and not have to work."

"It's good to have plans and dreams," said Jonathan, relieved at being able to deflect the conversation away from himself. "What would you like to learn to do?"

"I like carpentry," said Wolf. "I'd like to make furniture and make people's homes look nice."

The three continued to chat easily. But Jonathan was to recall his exchange with Sorele just a few days later.

He was in the process of placing his violin carefully in its case at the end of the evening when Mr. Kowalski approached him. It was quite late and there were few diners left in the restaurant.

"Jonathan, would you like to join me for a glass of tea. There's something I'd like to discuss with you."

Jonathan seated himself at a table as one of the two remaining waiters served him and Mr. Kowalski a glass of tea.

"Jonathan, I want to talk to you seriously about Sorele." Jonathan's heart sank, knowing what was to come.

"She's spoken to me about you and what she has to suggest seems reasonable. In fact, it seems a very good idea to me." Jonathan attempted to look interested instead of terrified. "Jonathan," continued Mr. Kowalski, quite unaware of the real effect he was having on his employee, "Sorele likes you." He paused, waiting for some reaction from Jonathan.

"She's a very pretty girl, Mr. Kowalski," said Jonathan.

"She's a bright girl, too."

Jonathan seriously considered upsetting his glass of tea to distract Mr. Kowalski from his subject. But that would be too obvious, he thought. There was no escape.

"Now, Jonathan, do you like her? Do you care enough for her to share your life with her? I would make sure you were both comfortable. For a start, you could help me run this place. For sure, there's enough work here for two, and we could even expand the business."

Jonathan said nothing, playing for a little time.

"So, Jonathan, what do you think?"

"It's a very interesting proposal. Mr. Kowalski." He paused. "But I need a little time to think about it. I still feel very close to my dear wife of blessed memory," he lied "and I also miss my family. Please, could I have a few days to think about this?"

"Take all the time you need, dear boy. I know you don't want to rush into anything, especially if you're not ready. Life is all a matter of timing," he said with a paternal pat of his stomach. "Just let me know as soon as possible," he added, contradicting himself.

Jonathan took his violin and went up to his room. Once again he felt pressured into accepting a match to which he was completely unsuited. Marriage. Why did everyone have to get married? And he could hardly refuse. How could he continue working for an employer whose daughter he had rejected? He became angry. He had finally created a niche for himself where he felt at ease, his own person, obliged to nobody, and now, once again, he found himself in precisely the situation he had run away from in Rypin.

As his exasperation subsided, he realized that this would be the pattern of his future life. Until he reached a certain age, he would be seen as most eligible, prey for any designing parent with a daughter who could provide grandchildren. So be it, he thought. Change would become the one constant in his destiny. He determined to concoct an excuse to refuse Sorele's hand, and to move on and away from Poznan.

The following evening, as the last diners left, Jonathan asked Mr. Kowalski for a few moments to talk to him. The two men sat at an empty table.

"Mr. Kowalski," he said, "Sorele is a beautiful girl and will make any young man a wonderful wife and a mother to his children. But our conversation last evening set me to thinking. I left Malbork to escape my memories. That's why I came to Poznan. But now I miss my family and I need some time with them to help me recover from my loss. So I have decided to return to Malbork for a while. Perhaps one day I'll come back to Poznan. But I would not want Sorele to wait for me. I'm sure there are other young men in this big city who would eagerly want to marry her, and without the complications that I would bring to our relationship."

"I'm sorry to hear that, Jonathan. I think you're making the wrong decision. Sorele will be so disappointed. I'm disappointed. The regulars in our restaurant will be disappointed. Your music, you know, adds a great deal to the atmosphere here. The place won't be the same without you."

"Forgive me, Mr. Kowalski. But the last thing I would want is to look at your daughter and see my Naomi's face." My Velvel's face, he thought. In his mind, he also prayed that Naomi was well and that his dishonesty would not cast the evil eye upon her. "It's time for me to move on, to go home."

"But perhaps you could forget about my daughter and just carry on as before, playing in the restaurant and going to the yeshiva."

Jonathan realized that he would never feel comfortable, having refused to marry his employer's daughter.

"No, Mr. Kowalski. Your proposal made me understand what I really want. I'm truly sorry. If you agree, I'll wait until Sunday and then leave."

"Of course, Jonathan, as you wish. You're a free man."

The few remaining days Jonathan spent with the Kowalskis in Poznan were a trial. The atmosphere at the dinner table was tense and the conversation rarely included him. Sorele studiously avoided his eyes. For his part, Jonathan had no intention of returning to Rypin. Such a decision would cause unnecessary pain to everyone. He decided that his chances of success would be best served in Warsaw with its huge Jewish population. But he let the Kowalskis believe that Malbork would be his destination.

His final performance at the restaurant was on the Thursday of that week. As usual, many diners had come to meet with their friends before the last day of the workweek before shabbes, which they spent with their families. Over time, Jonathan had become familiar with the faces of the regular patrons of the restaurant, even exchanging banter with them between his performances. He felt he owed them an explanation for his impending disappearance. He chose his moment after lowering his violin for the last time.

When the applause had died down he said, "Ladies and gentlemen, I have a sad duty to perform. You have just heard, or should I say that I have just been privileged to play my last performance in your beautiful city of Poznan." A chorus of 'nos' greeted this surprise announcement. Jonathan held up his hand. "Please allow me to explain. My aim in coming to Poznan was to recover from a personal tragedy, to escape a situation that was too painful to bear, the loss of my dear wife. Thanks to our wonderful hosts, the Kowalskis, and thanks to you all, I have now achieved my goal. I can now look to the future instead of the past, and the time has come for me to return home to my family…" At the thought of his parents and sisters, Jonathan stifled a sob. "… to my family whom I have missed for so long. So I thank you for your most warm appreciation of my humble efforts. And although I shall once again be where I belong…" He paused. Where may that be? he thought. "I shall miss you all very much. Thank you again."

His faithful audience erupted in cheers and good wishes as Jonathan placed his precious violin back in its case. You are my only true friend, he thought, and you are all I can rely upon.

On the Saturday night, after *havdalah,* the blessings over wine, a braided candle and spices marking the end of the Sabbath, in the Kowalskis' apartment, Mottl Kowalski paid Jonathan his last wages and wished him good luck. Jonathan went up to his room and packed his bags. He thought about his future. This would be the pattern – uncertainty followed by periods of temporary stability, an impermanent life to preserve a permanent lie. He wondered whether a time would ever come when people like him and Velvel could live together openly. He felt like an invisible pariah within the Jewish community, just as a Jew who dared venture into the non-Jewish world was made to feel in a more obvious way. Beyond the shtetls and city ghettos lay a hostile world for any Jew obliged to deal with it. And every observant Jew was immediately recognizable by the way he dressed. At least, thought Jonathan, here I can blend in with the people around me.

Early on the Sunday morning, Jonathan left the restaurant. None of the Kowalski family was there to bid him goodbye. His thoughts drifted back to his arrival in the city on the bumpy, noisy stagecoach with Abraham Pinsky. So much had happened… Herschel, Hermann, his success as a musician at the restaurant. In the outside world, too, life had changed radically. Few stagecoaches plied the roads of East Prussia, having been transplanted by the steam train. Jonathan's carriage deposited him quickly at the busy railway station, crowded with bustling passengers and their well-wishers. Jonathan traveled alone. As the train pulled away from the platform and left Poznan, he thought of all the people he had encountered: if they only knew.

Velvel, if they only knew.

Postscript

Silence filled the room. Transfixed by the story I had just heard, I looked across at Yankl, whom I now thought of as Jonathan. Despite all the challenges that he had confronted on a daily basis, his face shone with a sort of pride at having had the strength to control his life within the restrictions of his community. How easily I could have been him, I thought, had I been born a hundred years before my time.

"I really admire you," I said. "You refused to become a victim of the system; you were a survivor. But did you ever find happiness after your relationship with Hermann?"

"For two brief moments in my life. I had relations with a man. But we were like prisoners condemned to death. We could never have lived openly together. And a long-term close friendship would eventually have aroused suspicion. Fear ruled our lives. We saw ourselves as cripples with the constant threat of being cast out hanging over us."

"Did you ever hear from your family?"

"Yes, but not from my parents. I wrote them many letters. After Herschel passed away, I found another chevrusa who agreed to let me put his name on my letters as a return address. I told him I had done something bad in my hometown and didn't want to be traced. He was kind enough to accept my tale without question. But there was never a reply from my parents. Years later, by chance I met a man from Rypin. He had not heard my story but he knew my sister, Esther. She had married the son of the owner of the general store – a very good *shidduch,* match. I wrote to her and she answered me. She told me what happened after I left home.

"My parents were, of course, completely broken by my departure. My mother aged ten years, but she realized that she must put on a show of recovery for her two daughters' sake. My father refused to mention my name ever again.

"After Esther married, my mother revealed my entire story to her, from my love affair with Velvel, to his letter to me that she burned, but which finally convinced her that two men could love each other, to her appeal to Rabbi Levy not to excommunicate me, which later proved so ineffective. For years, my mother had bottled up her feelings about me and my life, and she finally confessed everything to Esther, to whom she felt very close. Esther, too, had rejoiced when my mother told her of my name change.

"Esther also told me that Rivka, my other sister, had married the shoemaker and after a few years and having given birth to a child, they emigrated to America. Her husband eventually opened a shoe factory in New York and became very wealthy."

"And Naomi?"

"Naomi married a few months after I left. She was very happy and had six children."

"Finally, Velvel. What became of Velvel?"

"Velvel was forced into a marriage. Esther told me that he and his wife had one child, a boy, whom they called Yankl. When I heard that, I was so touched that I cried. He had not forgotten me. But then, Esther told me, after three years he left his wife and child and immersed himself in his studies. He took little personal care of himself and was regarded as a recluse."

"I suppose you never saw him again."

"Actually, I did. Over twenty years after leaving Rypin, I visited Vilna. I was there to play at a *chassaneh,* a wedding, just after Succos, and I went to shul. At the end of the service, I saw a man a few rows in front of me. When he removed his tallis, there was something familiar about his posture that reminded me of Velvel. But he was bald with a fringe of hair that was almost white. Yet there were a few wisps of reddish hair remaining. I went up to him. He was engrossed in folding his tallis and putting it into a bag.

'Velvel?'

He turned toward me. His face was wrinkled, his eyes dull. All that remained of his former features were his eyebrows, still well defined and still red.

'Yes,' he said.

'Velvel Gambiner? It's me.' I recalled my former name: 'Yankl.'

For a moment, a spark flickered in his eyes. 'Yankl? I used to know a Yankl years ago in Rypin. Is it you?'

'Yes, it's me.'

'It's been a long time. A long time...' He looked at me closely. I too had aged, my dark hair and beard flecked with grey.

'How are you, Velvel?'

'Thank God, I'm surviving.'

'Surviving?'

He placed his tallis bag on the bench beside him.

'Surviving.'

I could feel his defensiveness. He had been alone too long and the wall he had erected around his life was too high. The bond we had shared had been broken.

'I hope you're well, Velvel.'

'Well? Yes, I'm well.' He paused. 'Where's my tallis bag?' he said, distractedly. 'Forgive me. I must go home.'

I picked up his bag from the bench and handed it to him. He walked slowly toward the door.

'Wait, Velvel. Wait.'

Velvel stopped in his tracks without turning around. 'What?' he said. 'What good can it do?'

'It's been so many years, Velvel. We should at least try and talk to each other. Come, sit down by me. Just for a few minutes.'

Velvel slowly returned to the pew in front of me and sat down, his back to me.

'I want to know, Velvel. I want to know what happened to you. Why are you… Why are you the way you are?'

'Must I relive it? Why should I tell you? What do you care? I wrote to you and you never even answered me.'

'Wrote to me? But Velvel, I never received a single letter from you. It must have been my mother who kept it from me. She was the one who would have received any letters at home. Try to understand, Velvel. I missed you so much. Do you really think I would not have answered any letter you sent me?'

Velvel slowly turned in his seat, his face toward me.

'Look at you, Yankl. You look so good, so young. You must be happy.'

'I am as happy as I could be, without you. There was only one way I could go. I left Rypin and made my life, such as it is. And you, what happened to you?'

Velvel sighed deeply. 'They made me do it. They made me marry her, my Zelda. I went through with it because I had no choice. I had no way to make a living and her father was well off. Somehow, soon after our wedding, she made me make love to her. It happened only once, and as a result, she became pregnant. We had a beautiful little boy. I named him after you, Yankl, and she never knew it. But I could not bring myself to make love with her again.' He paused, nodding his head slightly, his eyes closed, wallowing in the painful memory.

'Go on. Please go on, Velvel. I want to know.'

'She became abusive. She shrieked at me, accusing me of not caring for her, not loving her and not being a man. But how could I love her? How could I make love to her? She couldn't understand and I couldn't understand. Finally, I shut her out. I ignored her. I could not speak to her, and after a few weeks, she took the baby and went back to her father's house.'

'And then, what happened to you?'

'The apartment belonged to her father. I moved out and went to live in a room in the yeshiva. I explained that we were not compatible as husband and wife, and they asked no questions. Zelda's father came to see me and asked me what had gone wrong. I told the truth, that I could not make love to her, but I did not say why. That was just the way things were. So he asked me to give her a *get*, a deed of divorce, to which I agreed. Exceptionally, I had brought no financial assets into the marriage and I left without any. I even agreed not to try and see my son again. What could I do? I wonder how he's grown up. I heard Zelda remarried and I don't feel I have the right to interfere. My son, Yankl, probably knows Zelda's new husband as his only father.'

'Where are you living now, Velvel?'

'They gave me a room in the house of a widow who takes in boarders. I can at least shut the door and shut out the world.' He paused, unused to asking others about their lives. 'And you, Yankl, I see you've moved on…'"

Jonathan forced himself back into the present and looked at me. He sighed and continued his story. "I told Velvel briefly about my life and how I made a living. I made no mention of Naomi, Herschel or Hermann. Why upset him? Then we wished each other good health and good fortune and we went our separate ways."

"How did you feel when you said goodbye to Velvel?" I asked.

"Empty. I was overcome with emptiness. It swept through me from head to foot, like being slowly drenched in a spring shower. I sat in the shul for a few moments longer. I was shaken. All that emotion, all that hope, and now nothing. Perhaps it was better that way. I had lost him long ago, together with my family. But Velvel was my only true love. The relationship with Herschel was a coming together of like minds, and that with Hermann was based, above all, on physical contact. Both were, in their own way, incomplete, unlike that with Velvel."

Moments passed.

"But, you know, there was a sort of postscript to the last time I saw Velvel. There was no opportunity for us to speak again, but somehow, he found out about the wedding I was to play at. He came to the party after the *chuppah*, the wedding ceremony, although he had no invitation. I saw him at the back of the room, almost like a phantom and so out of place among the happy wedding guests. He nodded to me."

"Is that all?" I asked.

"No. My fellow performers and I finished the bulgar we had been playing, and then, as a solo, I played the *niggun*, the tune I had composed for him when we were together. As the melody gathered pace, I saw the tears roll slowly down his cheeks and, when it was over, the bow I gave the guests in response to their applause was for him. He knew it and gave me a small bow in return before he left the room."

I was moved. I empathized deeply with this long-lost cousin. His story was a tragedy that should never have happened, compounded by the loss of his family and hometown.

"Did you ever miss Rypin?" I asked.

"Of course, with every breath I took. I lived with the guilt of the anguish I had caused the people closest to me. But there was really no alternative. I could never have married Naomi. And those people, the ones I loved and respected the most, had taken Velvel away from me, the one person I could have loved. They hadn't even allowed us to say goodbye. When I think of that, I feel that I should be the one forgiving them."

I looked across the room, my expression full of sympathy.

"I wish I could have helped you. I wish I had known you."

"But you have and you do, better than anyone else," Jonathan replied. "This has been my catharsis. I am at peace."

I closed my eyes, offering a silent prayer for having been born more than a century after Jonathan into a kinder, more tolerant society. A faint smile played on Jonathan's lips. Then slowly his image faded and vanished.

Epilogue

January 2007. I had finally finished the first draft of my book. I thought of the characters I had created, the mothers and fathers, the sons and daughters, the rabbi, and of course, Yankl/Jonathan himself. Ordinary, unheroic people. I had felt their emotions, their joys, their distress and their reactions to a situation that was foreign to them, Yankl included. Nothing in their history or in their environment could have provided a map to help them navigate through their predicament.

In the background a radio was playing. I listened with half an ear as I revised some of my text. There was an interview with a professor from Tel Aviv University, and as always, the name of the city caught my attention. I listened more attentively. The professor's name was Eva Jablonka and her subject was a new science called Epigenetics. Epigenetics investigates the way in which potential is realized, including genetic potential. A major part of the science is devoted to the study of the transference of some potential-realizations down through the generations. Observations of the transfer of learned behaviors in several animal species, among other things, are used to illustrate the phenomenon.

I thought about this new science and my book. I recognized a similar pattern in Yankl's life and my own. We had both been under pressure to marry. We had both avoided the possibility by leaving home (although there had been other factors involved in my own decision). We had both mourned the loss of a lover, albeit the losses occurred for different reasons. We had both made a relative success of our professional careers. And we had both been blessed with an ear for music.

Those were the circumstances that we both dealt with in a similar fashion, in my case, as if resulting from epigenetic transfer through learned behavior. Of course, for me, the sense of heredity is stronger. I am convinced that someone like Yankl must have existed, and whenever my enthusiasm for writing his story waned, I could feel his finger jabbing my shoulder, and hear his voice saying: "Get on with it. We could not speak. You must speak for us."

So epigenetics, for me, is a powerful identification with the past and with a particular character in that past, imagined but entirely credible.

I have expressed that identification by offering a tribute to his bravery and his sacrifice, and to all those like him, rare and unsung as they may be. I salute all those who have refused to compromise their sexuality in order to adhere to the conventions of the day. Yankl may possibly have transferred his behavior to me. I have reciprocated by telling his story.

K. David Brody

For me, You have turned my mourning into dancing. You have loosened my sackcloth and girded me with gladness, so that my glory may sing praise to You and not be silent. My Lord, my God, I will give thanks to You for ever.

– Psalm 30

Glossary

The glossary below provides easy reference to the Yiddish and Hebrew words that are explained when first mentioned in the novel, and then forgotten. We all do it.

Aufruf – The custom for a groom to be called before the congregation to make a blessing when the final section of the weekly Torah is read in the synagogue. He then chants a section from one of the books of prophets.

Avoda zora – Idol worship.

Ayshes chayil – A tribute sung to the wife, mother and homemaker of the family, a woman of valor.

Bar mitzvah – The Jewish coming-of-age ceremony for boys. The bar mitzvah boy chants the weekly Torah portion and the reading from the books of prophets before the congregation.

Booba – Grandmother.

Brocha – A blessing.

Bulgar – A dance tune.

Challah – Braided egg loaf. Two of these loaves are blessed and eaten, partly or completely, at Sabbath meals.

Chanukah – An eight-day festival celebrating the rededication of the Temple after the Hasmoneans' victory over the ancient Greeks.

Chanukiyah – The eight-branched candelabra, lit on the festival of Chanukah, one more candle being lit every night of the festival.

Chassaneh – A wedding.

Chazzanut – Liturgical music.

Cheder – A Jewish school for children under the age of thirteen.

Cherem – A proclamation of excommunication.

Chevrusa – Study partner.

Cholent – A stew of beef, beans, egg and dumpling, carried to the baker on Friday before the start of the Sabbath and cooked overnight in his oven. No cooking is allowed on the Sabbath, so it was kept warm and picked up by children on Saturday morning and eaten at lunchtime on the Sabbath.

Chuppah – The wedding canopy and the marriage ceremony performed under it.

Davening – Praying.

D'var Torah – A short talk on a religious topic, often delivered outside the synagogue setting.

El molleh rachamim – 'God full of mercy', prayer recited by the cantor or rabbi at a funeral.

Esrog – Citron.

Gartel – A black cloth belt separating the spiritual upper body from the lower part containing the bodily functions.

Gefilte fish – Ground and boiled fish.

Get – A deed of divorce.

Gevalt – Disaster.

Havdalah – The blessings over wine, a braided candle and spices marking the end of the Sabbath.

Kaddish – The prayer for the dead recited by mourners.

Kashrut – Laws for the preparation and eating of kosher food.

Keriyah – The symbolic gesture of tearing a garment to express bereavement.

Kiddush – The reception following the shabbes morning service. Also, the blessing over wine.

Kittel – A white smock worn as a sign of spiritual purity.

Knaidlech – Matzah balls, eaten traditionally in chicken soup on Friday night, the Sabbath.

Kollel – Students in the yeshiva (seminary) who are married.

Lecha dodi – The congregational hymn sung on Friday evenings welcoming the Sabbath.

Loshon hora – Malicious gossip.

Ma'ariv – The evening prayer.

Mazel tov – Good luck.

Menora – Six-branched candelabra originally lit in the two Temples in Jerusalem.

Mezuzah – The ornamental casing containing a holy text placed on doorposts, as commanded in the Torah. The outward sign of a Jewish home or institution.

Mikve – The ritual bath used for spiritual purity.

Minyan – The quorum of men required for a mourner to recite the Kaddish, the prayer for the dead, and in order to hold any public religious service.

Mitzvah – A divine commandment.

Mommeh – Mother.

Momzerim – Bastards.

Naches – Pride and joy a person experiences from another, or from a happy event.

Niggun – A melody sung without words. Jewish mood music.

Ovel – A mourner.

Pesach – Passover.

Reb – A respectful form of 'Mr.'

Rebbitzin – The wife of a rabbi.

Ribonnoh shel olam - Master of the universe, referring to God.

Rosh Hashonahh – The Jewish New Year.

Shabbes – The Sabbath, Saturday, a day of complete rest.

Shadchan – A matchmaker.

Shammes – The beadle, the man handling minor organizational details in the synagogue.

Shaytel – The wig worn by married women out of modesty.

Shidduch – An arranged love match.

Shir hama'alos – The opening anthem for the grace after meals.

Sh'moneh esray – Literally, eighteen. The silent prayer, recited standing, although it actually contains 19 prayers.

Sholom aleichem/aleichem sholom – A greeting, meaning 'peace be with you'. Also, the first words of a traditional melody sung on arriving home after synagogue on Friday evening, and as legend has it, accompanied by angels.

Shtetl – A Jewish village.

Shtreimel – A wide-brimmed, round fur hat, worn by strictly Orthodox Jews on the Sabbath and holidays.

Shul – Synagogue.

Siddur – The Jewish prayer book.

Simcha – A family celebration.

Simchas Torah – The final day of the holiday season following Tabernacles marking the recommencement of the reading of the Torah cycle.

Shiva – Literally seven. The seven-day mourning period, excluding the Sabbath, to observe the loss of a loved one. Mourners sit on a low chair or stool, and family and friends visit to comfort them. Prayers are recited in the home when ten men are present.

Succos – The festival of Tabernacles when the custom is to eat (and even sleep) in flimsy booths reminiscent of the dwellings in which the Israelites lived for 40 years in the desert.

T'nach – The Bible.

Tallis – The prayer shawl.

Tatteh – Father.

Tefillin – Phylacteries, two small leather boxes containing a sacred text held with leather straps on the head and the left arm.

Shema – The holiest prayer recited at bedtime, upon rising and on other occasions.

Tikkun olam – The concept of repairing the world. Putting to rights what needs correcting, in partnership with God.

Tsitsis – A rectangular piece of cloth with a circular hole in the center for the head to pass through, and with four specially woven tassels on each corner. Male Jews are commanded to wear this garment as a constant reminder of the presence of God in their lives.

Yedid Nefesh – Soulmate. A haunting melody customarily chanted at the end of the Sabbath.

Yenta – A gossip.

Yeshiva – A Jewish seminary for males over the age of thirteen.

Yetzer hora – Any evil inclination, in this case, the sexual drive.

Yoh ribbon olom – God of the world, a Sabbath table song.

Yom Kippur – The Day of Atonement, a full day of fasting and the holiest day in the Jewish calendar.

Yomim noro'im – The days of awe between the Jewish New Year and the Day of Atonement.

About the Author

K. David Brody was born in London, UK. His grandparents immigrated to London from Rypin, Poland early in the 20th century and his parents were practicing Orthodox Jews. He graduated from Edinburgh University, Scotland, subsequently moving to Montreal, Canada, He worked initially at Société Radio-Canada, the French division of CBC, then moved to Jerusalem for two years in the 1980s. Although that experience was enriching from several points of view, it was there that he first felt truly Canadian. On returning to Montreal, he worked as a freelance translator from French to English. He continues to be an Orthodox Jew and participates actively in the Jewish community. *Mourning and Celebration* is his first novel.

Tell Your Friends!

We aren't a big publishing company, and we rely on word of mouth to get this book into the hands of new people. Can you help us to spread the word? Here are a just few things that you can do to help:

- ✓ Tell your friends and loved ones about the story that you've just read.
- ✓ Give a copy of the book as a gift.
- ✓ Visit our website and write a review. Even better, you can write a review of Mourning and Celebration on Amazon.com. <u>This will really help us</u>!

If you want to tell friends, we'd love to help. We've created a simple tool on our site that you can use to share this book with the people that you care about.

All you need to do is visit our site, and click on the "Tell Friends" navigation button. It's easy!

Thanks for all your help!

<u>www.MourningAndCelebration.com</u>

Made in the USA
Charleston, SC
04 February 2010